The Bard and the Gunpowder Plot

On the 400th anniversary of the Greatest Literary Hoax of All time

By Nick Kollerstrom, PhD

The Bard and the Gunpowder Plot

On the 400th anniversary of the Greatest Literary Hoax of All time

Contents

ISBN 978-1-7399994-4-5

A New Alchemy Press publication

2023

Acknowledgement: thanks to Stephen Windsor-Clive for inspiration and guidance; and to Bridgeman Images for permission to use portrait of William Stanley, Earl of Derby

Introduction

During the reign of Queen Elizabeth, Britain's Secret Service or if you like its intelligence agency was established, constructed primarily by Francis Walsingham (1532-1590) and William Cecil (1520-1598). Walsingham was a lawyer, politician, diplomat and spymaster, remembered as 'father of the British Secret Service,' while Cecil or 'Lord Burghley' as he was known had engineered the accession of Queen Elizabeth in 1558. He had much power during the history of the Tudor period.

The Catholic church which had been the religion of England for a thousand years was now illegal, banned totally. Instead the British monarch assumed the rather blasphemous position of claiming to be head of the Church. A sophisticated intelligence agency became necessary, to keep a check upon England's tormented Catholics and to detect any plots against the monarch that might appear.

After Walsingham passed away in 1590, William Cecil became the Queen's Secretary of State and his office became one of great power, second only to that of the monarch. After his death in 1598, his considerable skills as the country's chief intelligence officer passed onto his son Robert. The latter – who came to be called Lord Salisbury - was rather short and deformed having a twisted spine. He was not loved, it is safe to say. He may have been – or so we shall here argue - the chief creator of the Gunpowder Plot. Did he weave together its several cataclysmic themes that spelt doom - *permanent doom* - for Britain's Catholics?

William Cecil had a daughter Anne who didn't live very long (1556 – 1588) and she married Edward de Vere, the 'Earl of Oxford,' today the most favoured 'author of Shakespeare.'[1] She gave him three daughters and *each of these married or was engaged to a person to whom a 'Shakespeare' opus was dedicated.* That is *the primary link,* between the two deceptive stories which we here propose to narrate: the Gunpowder Plot and the Authorship of 'Shakespeare'.

Three and only three persons enjoyed this special privilege, of having works of 'Shakespeare' dedicated to them – one while he was alive, *Venus and Adonis* and then *The Rape of Lucrece* and of 1593 and 1594; and the other two after Shakespeare – *whoever he was* – had passed away, viz the complete *Works* of 1623, known today as the 'First Folio.' Each of these three dedicatees were married to or engaged to one of the daughters of the Earl of Oxford. Confused? You will be!

This fact has to be a major key to the vexed identity question.

The 400th anniversary of this publication, in 1623, is the occasion for the present work. However sublime its contents, of whatever immortal value it had and continues to have, it has to be judged as the greatest literary hoax of all time. How could these thirty-six plays, which express the very matter and story of Britain, be attributed to a person who could not even sign his own name? How come the supreme genius(es) who created this, the very English Renaissance, had to remain in the shadows?

At this point the weary reader may exclaim, Look, whole libraries have been written on this matter and don't seem to have gotten anywhere, can't we just leave it, can't we just enjoy the plays whoever wrote them? A reply here must surely be that the source of human creativity and genius is an interesting topic, and furthermore that it cannot fail to damage anyone's cognitive faculties to suppose that some illiterate and uneducated money-lender from Stratford – on - Avon somehow composed the whole thing.

Believing such a thing would be like, to give a modern analogy, believing that Osama bin Laden was responsible for bringing down the

---

1 That title doesn't mean he had anything to do with the city of Oxford. It's confusing. Properly he was called 'the Earl of Oxenford'

Twin Towers in 2001. Only quite dim people - I'd say - would believe such a thing. Or, they would reply, only conspiracy-theorists would *not* believe such a thing.[2] Thus we continue the eternal and in a way quite Platonic endeavour of ascertaining the difference between what is real and what is illusory.

Stratford-on-Avon is the very Mecca of English tourism but alas everything about it is bogus. On this 400th anniversary England should endeavour to abolish the Stratford-on-Avon tourist industry and to seek instead for where the plays were actually composed. We should reject the agnostic attitude of John Michell's '*Who Wrote Shakespeare?* which merely reviewed all of the candidates but could not reach any conclusion; and instead reach a collective, shared negative agreement that: *there never was a living human being called William Shakespeare who wrote plays, nor did anybody in Stratford-upon Avon ever write a play* - contrary to what Ben Jonson indicated in his Preface to the 1623 *First Folio.*

Stratford on Avon has been receiving some five million tourist visitors a year, with over 7,000 jobs servicing this industry. We live in a world based on unreal illusions.

Why would we want to juxtapose these two tremendous themes, of the Gunpowder Plot and the English Renaissance of theatre, the 'Works of Shake-Speare'? Is it a help to review them both together? The reader must judge. Both took place in a context of frightful persecution of anyone adhering to Catholicism. In both cases we find that major clues to What Really Happened were given by Jesuits, often French. In both cases we consult historical documents kept in the Public Record Office (the National Archives, in Kew) to refute the traditional story. In both cases quite a lot happens in Hackney, North London. A plaque there denotes a location of the Gunpowder Plot, but alas none there indicates that many of the immortal Shakespeare plays and sonnets were *probably* composed there.

2 N.K. *Who did 9/11?* 2018

Both events have exerted a central effect upon English culture. Both were given a fictional narrative concerning who did them, which must severely debilitate anyone's ability to evaluate historical causation. Also – and the reader may not like this bit – the Authorship Question or rather Answer becomes far more right-wing. We move away from Milton's rustic character who would 'warble his native woodnotes wild' - no, that really didn't happen – and come instead to an author or several authors very close to royalty. They live and have their being within the Tudor and Stuart royal courts. Likewise for the Gunpowder Plot, the King becomes not so much the intended victim but more, together with his intelligence officer, the instigator - the victims being rather the English Catholics.

Both stories have a connection with the palatial building on London's Strand, where the Cecil family lived. As a child Edward de Vere (whose father died when he was 12) grew up there, looked after by William Cecil. Edward was a cousin of the Queen and so a courtier from his earliest youth. The Gunpowder Plot 'villains' - or should we say chief protagonists - were espied by sundry persons coming and going from that building around the midnight hour...

Nobody will testify to seeing any gunpowder. "Its all in the mind" as John Lennon would say.

A new religion is invented with the King as head of the church, this being a total crucifixion of the teachings of Jesus. Henry 8th had sort of done that, announcing himself as head of the church as he confiscated all of the monasteries' wealth. The Gunpowder narrative reinforced this by creating a very strong duality between the King who, aided by Divine Providence, had rescued Britain from disaster by discovering the fiendish plot just in time - versus the Catholics who had allegedly schemed to blow up parliament. It becomes compulsory for clergymen to preach sermons about his event every year and for congregations to pray for the monarch. The wars against Spain are ratified and reinforced, after all it was a Catholic country.

The darkest Shakespeare plays such as *Macbeth* and *King Lear* appear in the immediate aftermath of this event.

Ben Jonson, England's first poet Laureate, is aware of both plots.[3] He had dinner with the Gunpowder Plot plotters a couple of weeks before the event. As a convert to Catholicism - he and his wife were dragged into court for not going to an Anglican church service – he was in a vulnerable position, partly because he didn't really believe the official story. He then as we'll see becomes probably the most central figure in the great 'Shakespeare' cover-up.

Henry Wriothesley (pronounced 'Roseley') the 3rd Earl of Southampton would have had quite a lot to say about both plots, had he wished to - but alas he didn't. To him were the very first works bearing the name of Shakespeare dedicated! That was in 1593-4: two long-winded, erotic sagas which no-one would read today but which were best sellers through the 1590s.The love expressed in these dedications was has been viewed as ardent and somewhat over-the-top. Wriothesley has to have known the identity of this author! What a shame he never published his memoirs.

Some years later, he was arrested together with the Earl of Essex, formerly the Queen's favourite but now accused (surely quite wrongly) of fomenting a rebellion against her.[4] Both were locked up in the Tower of London in February of 1601, and Southampton had to remain there until the Crown changed from Tudor to Stuart in 1603. Essex had been asking for an England of religious toleration without all the torture and persecution. Many of those arrested a few years later as 'gunpowder plotters' had supported Essex and were likewise arrested. From a modern point of view these were the good guys… Essex had no hope of

---

3 Richard Dutton, *Ben Jonson, Volpone and the Gunpowder Plot* 2012

4 He aimed to persuade the Queen to call upon parliament to ratify a Stuart Succession, thereby avoiding civil unrest and prevent Spanish rule. He was bravely supported by the Earl of Southampton but his enemy Robert Cecil outwitted them: Clare Asquith, *Shakespeare and the Resistance,* 2018, p.182. Or, he 'aimed at removing Robert Cecil from power.' (Whittemore, p.79)

clearing his name, however the life of Henry Wriothesley was spared, possibly because of behind-the-scenes activity by Edward de Vere.

Both narratives have their true natures only emerging around their quattrocentenary. This could be a process of self-knowledge and understanding for England. Two stupendous deceptions pop like bubbles. Instead, we may want to ask, what is the nature of genius and where does it come from? That profound question has been brushed under the carpet by a four-centuries long delusion, of a coarse money-lender as creator of the plays. Also, the endless horrible wars in which Britain has been involved, which have served to extinguish *all real culture,* require an intensity of hate against a perceived 'Enemy' *before* they can be fought. The Gunpowder Plot was I argue the first successful instance of such – the distance-projection of an illusory enemy-image by the King of England.

If our topic has a certain urgency, it comes from the way in which state-fabricated terror has been used extensively in this 21st century to ratify wars and tell people whom to hate. Is it not a major British art-form, a straight-from-Hell theatre?[5] It involves the concept of *the Villain*: who is evil, takes the blame and gets punished by death before he has the chance to give his point of view. The State controls the narrative. British intel creates a drama, which shocks everyone by its cruelty and inhumanity. It then projects the blame – that is the clever bit - onto a distant third party. And so we are led to reflect upon the nature of Evil. Guy Fawkes gets associated with Catholics, the Devil and the Pope. He is execrated for four centuries with his effigy burnt all over England once a year. I'm not quite going to say he was innocent *but* it is more or less impossible to ascertain what he thought he was doing on that November 5th. The Pope and all Jesuits get blamed, *as if* they had intended such a thing. A comic-book duality of good guys versus bad guys is set up, which tells us whom to hate.

In endeavouring to fathom these matters we become part of a 'truth' movement.

---

5 P. 136. N.K. *False Flags over Europe, A Modern History of State-Fabricated Terror*, 2018.

PART I

'William Shakespeare'

The curious case of the playwright who never existed

There lived in Stratford-upon-Avon a fellow called William Shaksper, who could not read or write. His parents could not read or write. His children could not read or write. He was quite successful, his father having been the town mayor and he acquired a house. He lent money with interest but otherwise practiced as a butcher or tanner. And, no, he didn't attend the local grammar school. No letters to or from him have ever been found. At his death no-one took any notice.

The plays attributed to 'William Shakespeare' make no mention of Stratford-upon-Avon or the countryside around it. One fellow searched though the homes within a fifty mile radius to see if anyone had a book that had belonged to Mr Shaksper. You know, maybe a play, that sort of thing? But to no avail. His will left his 'second-best bed' to his wife and gave no hint of any desk or writing equipment or books.

Thousands of books have been published upon the question of 'Shake-Speare' authorship and to sum things up it seems unlikely that any playwright of that name ever existed. It was more in the nature of a literary allusion, as in Minerva springing from the brow of Zeus shaking her spear – and representing *Inspiration.* Plays attributed to Shake-speare or Shakespeare started appearing before the Stratford character was old enough to have written them (if he could write), and these 'early plays' were judged to be not part of the authentic corpus.

There was in that time good reason for an upper-crust gentleman or especially someone close to royalty with an urge to write plays wanting to stay anonymous. Such a playwright could get tortured to death and indeed that did happen. Just look what happened to Marlowe. The 'Shakespeare' plays were appearing with no date or name attached to them. Clearly that was not very satisfactory and some name had to be found, and it did then appear years later with the 'First Folio' of the plays.

Somebody must have written them, after all.

There is no portrait of 'Shakespeare' in his lifetime, and the ones that did appear later have got a curiously disembodied head as if not portraying a real person.

The Stratford Fellow

Mr Shaksper was a successful businessman who worked in both Stratford and London: 'No-one who met him made a record during his lifetime of what he was like or what he said or did.'[6] He and his father applied for a coat-or-arms in 1596 and he did not then describe himself as a poet or playwright and perhaps in consequence the application was greatly delayed. He was merely a 'player' and actors had a low status, as in rogues and vagabonds or maybe brothel-keepers.

Two letters have been found mentioning his name, both concerned with money-lending.

There exist six signatures of Mr Shakspere, upon legal documents, three of them for his will. In 1985 a statement emerged from Her Majesties Stationary Office, reporting on Shakespearean documents held by the Public Records Office.[7] The Principal Assistant Keeper of Records Jane Cox commented upon this will, which was signed in three places:

---

6 John Michell, *Who Wrote Shakespeare?* p.53

7 J. Cox 1985, *Shakespeare in the Public Records* (HMSO); quoted in Michell p.100.

It is obvious that these signatures are not the signature of the same person. Almost every letter in each is formed in a different way.

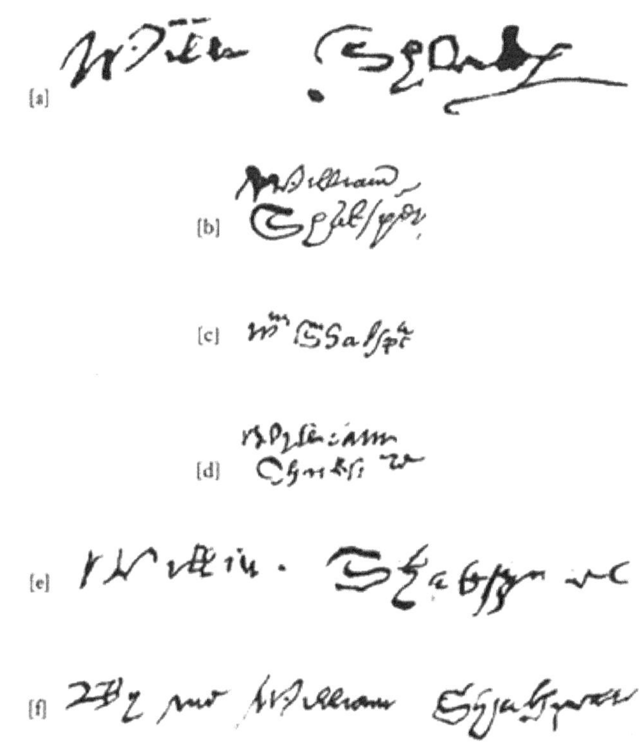

Figure: the six known signature of Mr Shaxpere

In her view these were by three different people. In other words, the Stratford character could not even sign his own name. In a letter to *The Times* in 1985 she went further, that

> The marked discrepancies between the signatures lend credence to the views of even the most extreme anti-Stratfordians. Could this man write his own name, let alone anything else?

They had been signed by the clerks who drew up the documents, she proposed. That was a significant turning-point in the whole debate.

The Stratford fellow married Anne Hathaway, who thus became *'Anne Shaxpere, wife unto Wyllyam Shaxpere'* as recorded in 1601. His elder daughter married in the name *Susanna Shaxpere* and his mother was *Mayry Shaxpere* in the record of her burial. At other times *Shaxbere* was used. *Shakspere* was the baptismal, burial and family name of the wealthy Stratford trader - a traditional English name - and *never once* did he use Shakespeare or Shake-speare. So many books have tried to blur this issue (NB it is well known that persons neither able to read or write are able to recognise their own name written down.)

The name 'Shaksper' was consistently used by the Midlands businessman while 'Shake-Speare' was consistently used by the writer – there was no overlap. Never did the author/playwright spell his name Shakspere. This period was a golden age for authors' pseudonyms and there was nothing unusual about it. It combined a verb and a noun, Shake-speare. (Thomas Vicars' 1628 description of 'that famous writer who takes his name from the shaking of a spear.'[8])

Figure 1: the Stratford man as shown in *Antiquities of Warwickshire,* reprinted many times[9]. The same drawing of Mr Shaksper clutching a sack (of grain?) upon his tomb- monument was reprinted in later, corrected editions.

8 3nd Edn. of his *Manual of Rhetoric*, 1628; quoted in Michell, p..
9 William Dugdale, *Antiquities of Warwickshire* 1730, p.520.

There was a gravestone put up for Mr Shakspere, seven years after his death, with a statue of him not looking in the slightest like a playwright, and holding a woolsack. Some years later an anonymous group of people from London arrived and insisted on carving out some verses upon his gravestone, attributing plays to him. Now that was a shocking thing to do. Soon after that came the chaos of the civil war and people's memories of what had been before that were hazy.[10] What they wrote wrongly averred that the corpse was buried within the monument (it may have been buried under the church floor) - perhaps not realising how incongruous their words would look in association with the crude effigy of a small-town tradesman:

> Stay passenger, why goest thou by so fast?.. within this monument Shakspeare ... sith all he has writ, Leaves living art but page to serve his witt.'

The inscription vaguely hints that Mr Shakspere was Shakespeare, partly by spelling the name 'Shakspeare,' while giving no details about his life or death. It would have been installed around the time of the First Folio and the first account of anyone noticing it was well after that date of 1623. The inscription would reassure anyone who came to Stratford as a visitor after reading the First Folio preface (see below), that indeed

10 A Titherley, *Shakepeare's Identity* 1952: see Michell, p.96.

here was the poet buried, while aiming on the other hand not to generate undue suspicion amongst persons who had known Mr Shakspere. Only a century later did it start to dawn upon Stratfordians what a genius had – allegedly - been in their midst.

Stratford monument adjusted, c.1623
- THE MONSTER HOAX -

The Stratford fellow Mr William Shakspere was born in 1564, married in 1582 and died in 1616. In 1596 he applied for a family coat of arms, then the next year he purchased a large house in Stratford.[11] In those same years he appears to have make a startling and almost miraculous appearance in London as part of a group of players. He may have been there as a trading agent for his father. The journey took several days on horseback from Stratford-on-Avon to London.

Shakspere became associated with the London theatre-companies primarily by (it is believed) financial loans, in the course of which he did come to act some minor parts, eg he is said to have acted as the ghost in *Hamlet*. Much later in 1635 a petition by Mr Shakspere's fellow actor Cuthbert Burbage alluded to Mr Shakspere as having been a business partner and an actor.[12]

A writ for Shakspere's arrest was issued in 1596, together with various other shady underworld characters: 'Be it known that William

11 A.J. Pointon, *the Man who was Never Shakespeare, the Theft of Shakespeare's Identity*, 2011, p.55.
12 Pointon p.164.

Wayte craves sureties of the peace against William Shakspere, Francis Langley, Dorothy Soer, wife of John Soer, and Anne Lee, for fear of death, and so forth. Writ of attachment issued to the sheriff of Surrey [29 November 1596].' The others mentioned seem to have been gangsters and racketeers. Francis Langley had previously been charged with violence and extortion. John Michell found the episode to be 'a squalid tale of rivalry among villains' which concerned 'control of the local vice trade and organised crime' in a region just south, the 'Surrey side,' of the Thames, where the Swan Theatre had just been built.[13]

Did he ever suspect that he would be credited posthumously with a vast literary enterprise? His receiving of the credit came well after his passing in 1616. Was there an inevitable fate with the proximity of his name, differing by a mere two letters?

Emergence of the Plays

The pseudonym was invented or first used for the bestselling political-allegory poem *Venus and Adonis* (1593), i.e that was the first publication to carry the name. The dedicatory epistles to both *Venus and Adonis* and then *Rape of Lucrece* 1594 were signed by 'Will Shakespeare'. [14] The latter was published with a poem prefixed by Henry Willobie that alluded to 'And *Shake-Speare* paints poor *Lucrece* rape.' The Bard was praised in the 1590s for *Venus and Adonis* but not for his plays, none of which were published under his name until 1597-8.

The plays start appearing around 1590. *Hamlet* is mentioned in a book published in 1589 and may have been written in 1587. 'too early' for the Stratford man. There is evidence for a *Timon of Athens* play in 1584, of a *Comedy of Errors* in 1577, a *Titus Andronicus* in the 1570s.[15] Later on, 'In 1598 the name Shakespeare or Shak-speare began appearing on the title-

13 Michell, p.249.

14 Clare Asquith, *Shakespeare and the Resistance, the poems that challenged Tudor Tyranny*, 2018.

15 *Romeo & Juliet* 1591, *King John* 1589-90, *Othello* usually put at 1603/4, but there is a pre-1600 reference in the 'commonplace book' of Edward Pudsey.

pages of plays, many of which had previously been published anonymously.'[16]

In 1594 the Lord Chamberlain's Men came into existence. They performed the plays.

The reign of Queen Elizabeth ended in 1603. Three well-known candidates for authorship are Christopher Marlowe, the Earl of Oxford and Francis Bacon and they die in 1593, 1604 and 1626.

The title-page of *The Life of Sir John old-castle* states that it was written by William Shakespeare (1600); likewise *The London Prodigal* by William Shakespeare (1605) and *the Yorkshire Tragedy* by W. Shakespeare 1608; the latter two were in the repertoire of The Kings Men, the actors who performed the Shakespeare plays.

The first play written by 'William Shakespeare' is reckoned to have been *Henry VI* of 1591 and remarkably it covered fifty years of international political relations, which hardly suggests a young author. This was the first of four plays, a tetralogy, covering the Wars of the Roses that were fought between the houses of Lancaster and York (Henry VI Part 1, Part 2 and Part 3 and then Richard III). Later on in 1597 *The Tragedie of King Richard the Second* was published with the name of 'William Shake-speare' – i.e., it was the first play to be definitely attributed to him.

A politically incorrect play was a risky thing. Thus in 1597 Ben Jonson was acting in a play *The Isle of Dogs,* considered to be seditious. He was thrown into jail and all copies of the play were seized and burnt - so no-one knows what the play was about! All theatres were ordered to be closed down for months afterwards as a warning. The other co-author Thomas Nashe managed to escape but all his papers were seized and burnt - and nothing else he might ever write was allowed to be published! The Crown held tight control over the printing presses.

By the year 1598 the Author was hailed as deserving immortal fame: 'Shakepeare thou, whose honey-flowing vein…' mainly for his *Venus and Adonis.*[17]

---

16 Michell p.52.

17 Richard Barnfield, *A Remembrance of some English Poets*, 1598, cited in Michell, p.55.

The Author of the Sonnets has to be dead by 1609, that being when they were published, with a tribute to 'our ever-living poet:' a phrase generally taken as implying that the author was no longer alive.

The first plays – a historical quartet?

agreed to be by 'Shakespeare'

'Wars of the Roses' 15th century

Henry VI Part 1	1591
Henry VI Part II	1591
Henry VI Part III	1591
Richard II	1592-4

aster Rose York Rose Tudor R

As early as 1584, a play was 'presented and enacted' for the Queen by Edward de Vere:

> Accounts of the Office of the Revels
> December 27, 1584
> "The History of Agamemnon and
> Ulysses, Presented and Enacted before
> Her Majesty by the Earl of Oxenford his
> Boys on St. Johns Day at night in Greenwich
> (Modernised English)

It is surmised that this play was the original version of what later became *Troilus and Cressida.*[18] It could well be 'the first play by Edward de Vere ever published.'[19] One critic surmised that 'this play may have been written by the Earl of Oxford himself, as he was known as one of the best dramatic writers of the day' and 'he was the only dramatic author of note.'[20] Gradually, as they were acted, the plays came into being. 'In due course these old plays, altered almost beyond recognition, with new thoughts, new knowledge and new words, came finally under the hand

18 G.W.Purdy, *Ulysses and Agamemnon (1584), The Early Plays of Edward de Vere* (William Shakespeare) Book 1.
19 Whittemore *op.cit.*, p.223.
20 Whittemore Ibid p.223, quoting Eva Clark *Hidden Allusions in Shakespeare Plays* 1974.

of the Master, and became known as plays by William Shakespeare.' (Evans, p.52)

In the 1590s records of *performances* of what would be later regarded as 'Shakespeare' plays begin to appear. Plays were becoming popular with half a dozen London theatres were normally open for six days a week, with maybe a couple of thousand persons watching reach performance. There were more than a thousand professional players in town and a couple of hundred amateur play writers. New scripts could be expected to last a couple of weeks.

Diary of the Rose Theatre manager Philip Henslowe:
gives the plays performed 1591-1609

It mentions all the well-known dramatists of the day (but NOT Shakespeare) plus how much he paid for each play

Some titles he records are Shakespeare-like, eg

Titus and Ondronicus	1593
King Leare	1593
Tamynge of a Shrowe	1594
hamlet	1594
Troyelles and Cressida	1599
Sesers Falle	1602 (=>Julius Caesar?)

Ten 'Shakespeare' plays are alluded to, but not as by 'Shakespeare'

The theatre manager Philip Henslowe recorded the newly-formed troupe of actors the Lord Chamberlain's Men doing a play called *Hamlet.*

A lot was happening around 1594, as the plays are appearing onstage. Here are some main events:

- May 1593 Christopher Marlow murdered & his friend playwright Thomas Kyd tortured.
- January 1594 *Titus Andronicus* was first performed, at the Globe Theatre.
- April 1594 Fernandino Stanley is poisoned; his brother W.S. becomes the 6th Earl of Derby
- Spring 1594 The theatres of London re-open after the plague outbreak of '93.

- May 1594 *The Rape of Lucrecia* registered for publication, by 'William Shakespeare'
- June 1594 Henslow diary records the production of *Hamlet*
- Summer of 1594 The Lord Chancellor's Men begin producing plays, and will remain Britain's top theatre company for the next forty years.
- December 1594 *The Comedy of Errors* was first performed, at Grays Inn Hall.
- January 1595 William Stanley marries Elizabeth the eldest daughter of Edward de Vere.

There then began a process of *publishing*. Eight plays were published separately having *no author's* name:

Titus Andronicus	1594	*Taming of the shrew*	1594
Henry VI Part II	1594	*Henry VI, Part III*	1595
Romeo and Juliet	1597	*Henry IV, Part I*	1598
Richard II	1597	*Richard III*	1597

The last two of these, Richard II and Richard III stated on their front pages: 'As it has been lately acted by the Right Honourable the Lord Chamberlain his servants.' Credit was thereby given to the actors, *not* to an author; or possibly to Mary Sidney and her husband, insofar as they were sponsoring 'the Earl of Pembroke's Men' as that company was formerly known. One could infer that the players themselves helped to shape the plays. Next, a trio of plays are published with title-pages having the name of the Bard but *not* claiming that he was the Author!

> *Richard the Third,* 1598: 'As it hath been publicly acted by the Right Honorable the Lord Chamberlain his servants, newly augmented by W. Shakespeare'
>
> *Loves Labours Lost,* 1598: As it was presented before her Highness this last Christmas, Newly corrected and augmented by W. Shakespeare'
>
> *Henry IV Part I* 1599 'Newly corrected by W. Shakespeare'

The adjustments between the first and second editions were slight, so 'newly augmented' or 'corrected' signified rather little.

Mediaeval artists did not wish to put their names on their paintings. The great Mediaeval cathedral-builders remained anonymous, so whatever they were working on they did not have an egoic motivation, of wanting their name attached to a work of art so it would be remembered. *Romeo and Juliet* appeared in 1597 anonymously and was called a 'monstrous theft' by certain authors.[21] Perhaps the author, the Bard, was not too concerned about where the elements of the play came from as likewise he didn't put his name to it.

Finally in 1598 a claim of authorship is made, for the second edition of the play *Richard II.*

'By William Shake-Speare'

has been added and it is *underneath* the credit which remains unchanged - as previously given - to the players. That's it! Finally, the World's Greatest Playwright puts his name - or a name - to a play. *And* it would have been immediately clear to anyone buying a copy that no person of that name existed.

In 1601, the play *Richard II* was performed at the Globe Theatre, by way of supporting the Essex rebellion, and the Lord Chamberlain's Men found themselves in hot water for putting on this play, seen as supporting monarchical overthrow. The Queen was furious as various people were beheaded. Persons were interrogated but never in this process do we hear of anyone hinting that it was a play by 'Shakespeare' - it was simply, *Richard II.*

When *Hamle*t was published in 1603 its Frontespiece stated: 'As it has been diverse times acted by his Highnesse servants in the Cittie of London: also in the two Universities of Cambridge and Oxford, and elsewhere' – with the name placed above, 'William Shake-speare.'

Surely, these title-pages are not telling us that an Author wrote the plays then gave out copies to the troupe of actors. The actors may have been illiterate: which means that they lived much more in the present tense, and in acting out the dramas helped to knock them into shape. After the actors had done that in one or two productions, somebody puts the name 'Shakespeare' to a written-out text.

---

21 K Chiljan, 'Why was Edward de Vere defamed on stage?' *The Oxfordian* 21, 2019 p.58

There is a case that the main plays were composed in the late 1570s when de Vere was around twenty-eight years of age. Then they were polished up, *finalised,* in that wonderful twelve-year period of silence, when de Vere retired to Hackney and the immortal name of Shakespeare first appears. They were worked upon gradually over decades:

The History of Error => Comedy of Errors

Agamemnon and Ulysses (1585) => Troilus and Cressida

History of the Second Helen => Alls well that Ends Well

A History of Ariodante and Genevora => Much ado about Nothing

The Famous victories of Henry V => Henry V

The Pleasant Conceit => Twelfth Night

History of the Solitary Knight => Timon of Athens

The Jew => The Merchant of Venice

A History of Titus and Gisippus => Titus Andronicus

A Moral of the Marriage of mind and Measure => Taming of the Shrew

During the life of Edward de Vere, a total of eight plays were published which declared that their author was William Shakespeare, and that was over a six-year period. Here the red colour indicates these plays.

THE EIGHT PLAYS 'BY SHAKESPEARE' PUBLISHED IN DE VERE'S LIFETIME

1603 Hamlet

1602 Merry Wives of Windsor

1601

1600 Much Ado about Nothing Merchant of Venice Henry IV, II A Midsummer Night's Dream Life of Sir John Oldcastle[22]

1599 Henry IV ,I

1598 Henry IV, I Richard III Loves Labours Lost Richard II

22 The *Life of Sir John Oldcastle* published in 1600 stated it was 'by William Shakespeare' which is not nowadays accepted. The character of Falstaff may have been based upon the historical figure of Sir John Oldcastle. The play published in 1600 – and later included in a 'folio' collection of the plays – could have evolved from one of de Vere's early works in the 1570s. He was in no position to object if anyone else used his *nom de plume.* That play was excluded from the First Folio of 1623.

1597 Romeo and Juliet Richard II Richard III

1596

1595 Henry VI, III

1594 Titus Andronicus Taming of the Shrew Henry VI, I

Anonymous Augmented/corrected by W.S.

'by William Shakespeare'

If we discount the John Oldcastle play as not being 'really' by Shakespeare, then there were *seven plays in de Vere's lifetime*, that were published as being 'by William Shakespeare.'

After the first publication of *Hamlet*, considerable modifications to the text appear a year later - evidently a result of King James' ambassador having sailed to Elsinore in Denmark in July of 1603 on diplomatic business. In 1604 the second edition appears, greatly enlarged and improved, with more exact details of Elsinore Castle, where the drama of the play was located. Thus the name of a courtier which had been 'Corambis' was changed to 'Polonius' (the Latinised form of Plönnies, an aristocratic Swedish name). Thus, the Author of the play had immediate access to Court information.

That is a very autobiographical play, if perchance its author were de Vere.[23] He became engaged to the daughter of Cecil, the Queen's chief intelligence officer; and likewise Hamlet was engaged to Ophelia the daughter of Polonius, who was the chief intelligence officer of the Danish queen. Hamlet was very cruel to Ophelia ('Get thee to a nunnery') and abandoned her: likewise de Vere cruelly refused to see his young wife for five whole years *after* she had produced his child - on a mere suspicion of infidelity.[24] She died very young maybe of

23 See Whittemore, *100 Reasons Shake-Speare was Earl of Oxford*, 2016, reasons 7-12.

24 For allegation that de Vere had not slept with his wife before leaving for Italy, see Anderson, Ibid, p.88. He was with his wife in October 1574 then departed for Paris on January 7th, then on 17th March he received the good news of his wife's pregnancy. He wrote to Cecil hoping it would be a boy: 'I thank God therfore with yowre Lordship that it hathe pleased him to make me a father…' Cecil kept that letter, when doubts began to assail the mind of de Vere. The problem was, de Vere was only informed on 24 September that his child Elizabeth had been born on 2 July. Then in April 1575 an Iago-type character arrives in Paris and tells him he's been cuckolded: the child had really been born in September when the letter was sent to him … See *This star of England* (Ogburn) for in-depth treatment. Could Elizabeth have married William Stanley were she illegitimate?

heartbreak, as did Ophelia in *Hamlet*. It has long been recognized that William Cecil was the model for Polonius: thus he formulated a list of precepts for his son (that were later published[25]) which are unmistakeably similar to those which Polonius reads out in *Hamlet*. De Vere's cousins Sir Horace Vere (sometimes called Horatio) and Francis Vere were both soldiers, reminding one of Hamlet's companions, Horatio and Francisco. Hamlet and de Vere were both patrons of play-acting companies.

Some feel that the dying cry of Hamlet -

> 'O God! – Horatio, what a wounded name,
>
> Things standing thus unknown, shall live behind me.'

Expressed the fate of Edward de Vere – whose biographers tend to concur that he had rather messed up his life! He had lost credit for his life-work for a start. The publication of the play *Hamlet* synchronised within weeks of de Vere's reported death in June 1604, after which all authorised publications of Shakespeare works ceased, until the First Folio of 1623.[26] The play ends with most of the main characters dead on stage, and that is the end - *Terminus est* - of the great flow of authorised-by-the-author 'Shakespeare' plays.[27]

Figure: the 'Shakespeare' candidate Christopher Marlowe.

25 W. Cecil, *The Counsell of a Father to his Sonne,* 1611.

26 'After 1604, the London stages and bookstalls appear to have been reviving bits and patches of a posthumous Shakespeare canon…When the King's Men appeared at court during the winter of 1604-5, Queen Anne [wife of James 1] requested that the company perform some Shake-speare that she hadn't already seen. They told her they could not fulfil her request. So the King's Men staged the old standby *Love's Labours Lost* instead.' Anderson, 397-400.

27 politicworm.com 'Oxford's death' reckons that he feigned his death and lived another 4 years: 'While supposedly dead he had nine plays ready for the marriage of his daughter to the younger Pembroke the following Christmas.'

Let's quote Thomas Looney here, as he was the first to twig what was going on. A hundred years ago, in his epic work of detection, he wrote: We have a flood of Shakespeare plays being published authentically right up to the death of Edward de Vere then a sudden stop, and nothing more published with any appearance of proper authorization for nearly twenty years…'[28]

The timelines in this diagram suggest that Marlowe died too young to be a candidate. Or, if it is supposed his death was faked – as it might well have been, to avoid a serious charge against him of atheism that was pending – then what? Did he write the plays in Holland? The plays seem to have emerged from actual situations and dramas in life, British royal life in particular. Marlowe did not live close to royalty and would not have known all about falconry – quite part from dying too early. The Bard, the real Bard, has to be present at the court of King James in 1604 to talk to the ambassador who had returned from Elsinore castle in Denmark.

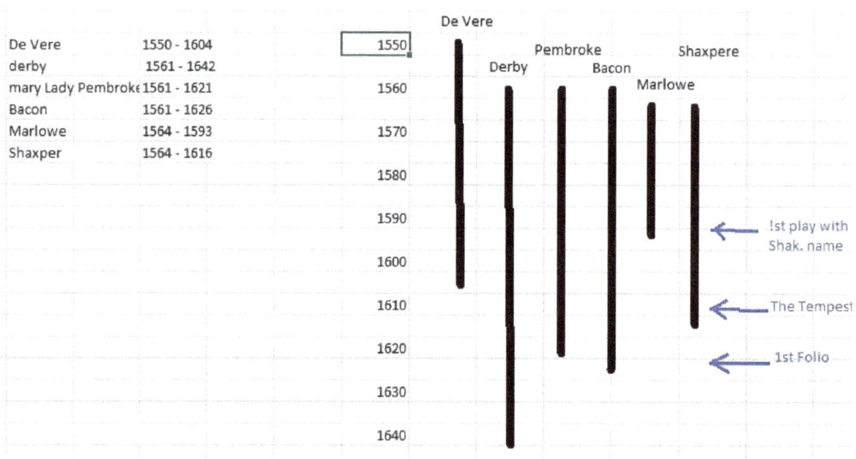

A Second Folio appeared in 1632, when all the main protagonists except for William Stanley had passed away. It had all the same plays but there were nearly two thousand amendments and improvements and who had done these? It correctly printed the 'u's and 'v's which had been interchangeable in the First Folio. John Rollett (in his *William Stanley as Shakepeare* p.34) reckoned that the original Author must have

28 Looney op.cit., 2018, p.357

been at work and he cited these two examples. *Romeo and Juliet* has the lines where Romeo first claps eyes upon Juliet: 'O, She doth teach the very torches to burn bright! / It seems she hangs upon the cheek of Night / Like a rich jewel in an Ethiop's ear. In the Second Edition the second line is altered: 'Her beauty hangs upon the cheek of night…' In the historical play *Henry VI* there is 'I will, and like thee, / Play on the lute, beholding the Townes burne' and this became in the second Edition 'I will, and Nero-like will…' (Henry VI, Act I, Scene 4, 95-6). These are substantial adjustments, and was it not the Bard himself making them? That could only have been, Rollett concluded, William Stanley (1561 – 1642).

Lord Bacon

Figure 6: Francis Bacon, the Lord Chancellor of England

Francis Bacon was one of the most brilliant intellects of all time and had an encyclopedic knowledge. He was one of England's top legal experts and there is a great deal about law in Shakespeare. Years later, Bacon became *the* philosopher for the scientific revolution in the 17th century. His prosaic style, about facts, learning and gathering evidence, is I suggest greatly opposed to fantasy and story-telling. When once he was giving advice about why one should study history (to a Mr Fulke Greville) he stated: "I think history of most, and I had almost said only, use. For poets, I can commend none, being ever resolved to be a stranger to them."[29] That accords (I suggest) with how people have viewed his work.

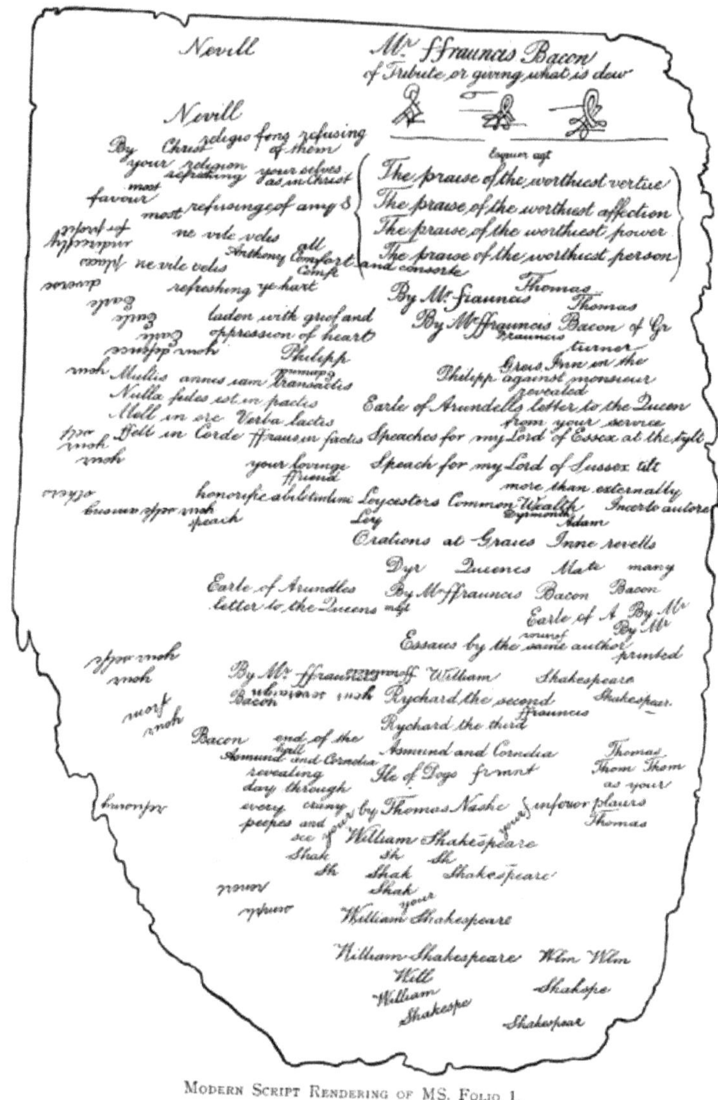

MODERN SCRIPT RENDERING OF MS. FOLIO 1.

Figure: The Northumberland manuscript, plus close-up

29 Bacon *The Major Works,* Ed. Vickers, 2002, p.105

By Mr ffrauncis William Shakespeare
Bacon Rychard the second Shakespear
ffrauncis
Rychard the third

Looking at his picture we see a lawyer and philosopher but surely not a romantic poet. In the course of his legal duties, he was not above putting an old man on the rack and stretching him, to try and obtain a confession; even of something that the fellow had not actually done![30] Such use of torture doesn't quite sound like the Author we are looking for.

He would have overseen the publication of the first Folio 1619-21 and given instructions, but could he really have been the author? His *Works* comprise many bulky volumes and these seem quite enough for one lifetime.[31]

What is called the 'Northumberland Manuscript' is all that remains of a file or folder belonging to Francis Bacon, believed to have been compiled around 1596-7. A transcribed version here shown, as being more legible than the original. We see Bacon's name at the top together with titles of various essays of his and allusions to the Queen. The name of Shakespeare appears at the bottom many times, plus there is allusion the first two plays to be published (1597-8) under the name of 'Shakespeare,' *Richard II* and *Richard III*. Bacon as the cousin, friend and literary colleague of de Vere the Earl of Oxford could have been assisting in their publication.[32]

The Manuscript quotes a line from the *Rape of Lucrece* poem 'revealing day through every cranny peeps.' It also quotes the extremely long latin word 'Honorificabiletunine' used in *Love's Labours Lost* – a play acted in 1597 and printed in 1698.

Just three words appear on the back of this manuscript: 'put into type' – indicating that it was Bacon's business to publish whatever had

30 Lord Macaulay, *An Essay on Francis Bacon* 1837 (online).
31 For a different view, see sirbacon.org/shakespearecircle.htm by Peter Dawkins.
32 Northumberland House is located next to Trafalgar Square. Francis Bacon lived next door

been in the folder, or at least to get it printed. No doubt he did this. Normally the person who does that, isn't the author.

This page alone rules out any Stratfordian context for authorship.

A Shadowy Identity

All references to 'Shakespeare' in the 1590s are references to a pseudonym that appeared on printed poems in 1593 and 1594 and on plays from 1598. They are not allusions to a real, living writer called 'Shakespeare.' – Alexander Waugh

It was understood among actors that Shakespeare's name on a play meant that the real author wanted no questions asked and it was in their interest to oblige him. It was convenient to have a stock name to attach to plays which for whatever reason the real author did not wish to acknowledge. It was evident that 'Shake-speare' was a pseudonym because there was no-one of that name in the literary circles of England. That is relevant to the delay in publication.

Prior to the First Folio, around half of the published plays had the author's name spelt 'Shake-speare.'

No literary people - with the exception of Ben Jonson - ever claimed to have known Shake-Speare: 'Jonson's comments on other writers, e.g. Drayton, Marston and Sidney, leave one feeling that he had actually seen them in person, but he left no hint that he had ever met either Shakspeare the actor or the man behind the pseudonym "Shakespeare."'[33]

No manuscript of a play or poem exists in his own handwriting. He is a *very* phantomic character. The World's Greatest Playwright knew how to maintain a low profile! There is no record of anyone paying 'Shakespeare' for his plays. The literary references to him in his lifetime 'were always to the author of poems and dramas, never directly to the man.'[34]

33 Pointon, p.109
34 Michell, p .54.

There were two characters who *knew*: Francis Bacon and Ben Jonson. Whatever the secret was, they died knowing it …

In 1614 Ben Jonson let slip an allusion to the Author in the preface to his play *Bartholemew Fair*. The characters they are about to watch have no hidden identities, he reassures his audience. They will not need to wonder about 'what concealed statesman [is meant by] by the seller of mousetraps' – an allusion to the play within a play of *Hamlet*, called The Mousetrap.[35] Jonson became in 1616 the Poet Laureate so 'Shakespeare' was so to speak his chief rival.

The Shakespeare play *Troilus and Cressida* was published in 1609. The anonymous printers boasted as to how they had wrested it from its 'proud possessors' – 'whoever they were.'[36]

A book published in 1622 (*The Complete Gentleman* by Henry Peacham) listed what it claimed were the seven greatest deceased writers of the Elizabethan era. The seven were Edward, Earl of Oxford, Lord Brockhurst, Lord Paget, Sir Philip Sidney, Sir Edward Dyer, Edmund Spenser and Samuel Daniel. Was 'Shakespeare' not considered to be an author, or was he perchance one of those mentioned? Many of the plays had been produced by then and surely he could not be ignoring them? Was one person on his list, eg Edward Earl of Oxford, that Author?

The Conspiracy is Launched: First Folio Preface, 1623

Ben Jonson may have worked as a secretary for Francis Bacon and thereby oversaw the publication of the First Folio in 1623 - a huge nine-hundred page book containing thirty-six plays, eighteen never before printed. There were no dates or sequence of composing the plays indicated nor any personal remarks from the Author.

Ben Jonson was evidently chosen to manage the great deception. The preface hinted that the illustrious Author was the man buried at

35 Asquith, *Shadowplay* p.263
36 Pointon, p.112.

Stratford but did not actually say that: 'to the memory of my beloved, The AUTHOR Mr. William Shakespeare and what he hath left us' he wrote, adding the memorable epithet 'sweet swan of Avon.' Thus he managed to imply that the playwright was the man from Stratford, as he endeavoured to give the publication which he pulled together - by a mystery author - a good send-off.

His preface hinted at the identity of 'Shakespeare' the mystery author, alluding to the bogus Stratford monument inscription. It was clearly implied that the Author was dead, which rules out Francis Bacon as a candidate:

> " ... the clever hints in the First Folio about Shakespeare being Shakspere involved a deception orchestrated by Ben Jonson. It is clear for instance that he wrote a poem for inclusion in the first folio to bestow fictional praise on a fictional portrait of the author. Also ... it is clear that Jonson wrote pieces which he then had printed over other people's names – those of John Heminges and Henry Condell – because these were former colleagues of Shakspere.[37]

Heminges and Condell were a couple of the 'Shakespearean' players who could probably not read or write. Jonson's deceptive Foreword created the impression that it was those two who had collected and edited the plays.

What legal right was there to publication? The editors were 'secretive and mendacious' as regards how they had obtained the texts or from what originals had they worked.[38] The deception was only launched after two actors who had known him, Henry Condell and John Heminges (neither known to have written anything), were both either dead or too old to object to tributes being falsely written in their names ... as if it were they who had collated the plays!

"I therefore will begin. Soule of the age! The applause! Delight! The wonder of our stage! *My* Shakespeare rise" effused Ben Jonson: was he here indicating a difference between the writer's pseudonym and the true author?'[39] He praised 'the AUTHOR' of the plays as being 'gentle'

---

37 Pointon p.9.
38 Michell p.80.
39 Alexander Waugh,

i...e. of 'noble' birth and, cryptically, not having a grave: 'Thou art a monument without a tomb.' Edward de Vere had and indeed has no known grave. The 'without a tomb' phrase argues against the Stratford identity. His Preface continued:

Sweet swan of Avon! What a sight it were
To see thee in our waters yet appear,
And make those flights upon the bankes of Thames
That so did take Eliza and our James!

alluding to the two monarchs Queen Elizabeth and James who had enjoyed having the plays enacted for them at Hampton Court Palace. Its Great Hall, which stood on the banks of the Thames, had in earlier times been called 'Avon.' Thus the poet William Camden who was Jonson's friend and mentor wrote: 'A stately place for rare and glorious shew / Times past, by name of Avon men it knew' (1610).

Jonson's phrase was certainly hinting at Stratford-upon-Avon, implying in his Foreword that the Author was born there, but without being mendacious or using anything that could incur legal action: 'every opportunity in the First folio for an unambiguous statement about Shakspere being Shakespeare had been carefully avoided.'[40] For example, Mr Shakspere had obtained a family crest, used on his Stratford monument and this would have been appropriate here would it not? But Jonson did not wish to use it.

The Author wrote for the aristocracy and must have been close to British royalty. There are for example many references to falconry, the sport of kings: 'There are 80 separate technical allusions to the sport [falconry] in his published writings, whereas there are few in the work of any other dramatist.'[41] He has in contrast hardly anything about the more working-class hobby of eg fishing, that hardly gets a mention. Of the thirty-six plays, only three have no king, emperor, prince or duke as main characters.

The former British politician Enoch Powell concluded that the plays displayed a close experience of the monarchy and of political power:

---

40 Pointon p.125.
41 Pointon p.176.

> They [the plays] are written by someone who has been part of the life of politics and power, who knows what people feel when they are near to the centre of power…That is not something which can be transferred, it's not something on which an author can be briefed. It comes straight out of experience, it come straight out of personal feeling.[42]

Asked concerning the bust in the Stratford church (figure 2b), Enoch Powell replied: 'I don't think it's the face of a man at all… It's a mask, to conceal an identity.'[43]

Figures: two fake 'Shakespeare' images. The first is from a 1640 reprint of the Sonnets ('a curiously disembodied head'); the second is monument at Stratford-upon-Avon after it had been altered in 1747 (quill pen added!), replacing that shown on page 11.

That insight by Enoch Powell is *so* important as regards the identity of the Bard. Thus we find -

> He (the Bard) wrote almost exclusively of courts and aristocratic life; and matters of state, of law, of kingship,

42 Enoch Powell: youtube, 'The Shakespeare Mystery' at ten minutes, 25.3.14.
43 Ibid at 25 minutes.

> and of dynastic succession are always prominent parts of his dramatic matter. This is true even in his comedies ... but it is even more obviously true in Shakespeare's history plays and in his tragedies, where the political issues are the very substance of the plays, and where crucial matters of state are explored with remarkable precision and in great depth.
>
> All ten of Shakespeare's English history plays are named after politicians...And they're all about the same thing: who gets to rule... The plots are political plots (literally plots) - assassination, treason, civil war, foreign conquest .. If ambition seems to be a universal aspect of political life, so too does the concept of 'legitimacy', which is the most salient theme of the English history plays. At stake in these plays is the question not only of who will rule, but of who is supposed to rule...[44]

De Vere, as a young man of twenty-two, wrote an introduction to an Italian book about Courtiers. Here's what he said:

> For what more difficult, more noble, or more magnificent task has anyone ever undertaken than our author Castiglione, who has drawn for us the figure and model of a courtier, a work to which nothing can be added, in which there is no redundant word, a portrait which we shall recognize as that of the highest and most perfect type of man... [No matter how] elaborate the ceremonial, whatever the magnificence of the court, the splendour of the courtiers, and the multitude of the spectators, he [Castiglione, author of *The Courtier*] has been able to lay down principles for the guidance of the very Monarch himself.'

He was himself a courtier, having been brough up at court, and here foreshadows the substance of plays he would later write. This Introduction was viewed a significant piece of literature. His Cambridge friend Gabriel Harvey reckoned it was better than the book itself! ('... that courtly epistle, more polished even than the writings of Castiglione himself...')[45] This Italian author had, de Vere wrote, created *'a new glory*

---

44. Whittemore *100 Reasons*, p.152, quoting A.B.Kernen, *Politics, Power and Shakespeare* 1981 and T.Spiekerman, *Shakespeare's Political Realism* 2001.
45 Whittemore, p.56.

of language ... For who is clearer in his use of words? Or richer in the dignity of his sentences?' That so well describes what he himself would later accomplish.

Chapter 2:

How The 'Shakespeare' Identity was used

The 'Magic Circle'

The Bard had a Jesus-like ability to avoid detection in the historical record, as if he glided through it leaving no trace, or virtually no trace. Ah, how many have searched for the identity of the man who sat down and composed the thirty-six plays! Perhaps no such person can be found because he never existed. We should take care not to ascribe too much to one individual. Instead, it will help to hear a view of the authorship question propounded almost seventy years ago by Alfred John Evans in his classic *Shakespeare's Magic Circle* of 1956. It still reads as the best account, viewing the creation-process as having been at least *at some stage* a collective, group activity:

> Surely there can never have been in any land an aristocratic clique which possessed such an exalted standard of education and culture as the Elizabethan upper classes – Oxford, Edmund Spenser, Sir Philip Sidney, Sir Walter Raleigh, the 4th Earl of Derby and his sons William and Ferdinando, Rutland and Lady Rutland (Sidney's daughter), Southampton and Lady Pembroke (Sidney's sister) to

name but a few. And to this galaxy of talent must be added the towering figure of Francis Bacon, who was intimate with them all. We know astonishingly little about their private lives; but they impress themselves on our imagination as picturesque, explosive, enthusiastic, impatient, creative, artistic individuals, very young and very much alive, living in a dangerous and exciting age. In 1588 for instance, shortly after the return of Stanley, the Armada sailed up the Channel and was defeated. Oxford fitted out a ship of his own and took part in the fray, and it is believed that William Stanley sailed with him. Drake and Raleigh were scouring the oceans, carrying on what amounted to a private and piratical war of their own.

These great men, though some violent quarrels are recorded, were mostly excellent friends and, as they met often at Court, were all well known to each other. They frequently visited each other's houses and Wilton House on the Salisbury Avon, the home of the Earl of Pembroke, was a favourite meeting place where drama and poetry were the subjects of greatest common interest and entertainment. They were nearly all scholars and linguists and many of them also concealed poets. They spoke or read Latin and French with facility and some of them had good knowledge of Italian and Greek as well. It is my belief *that it was by the interplay of wit, knowledge and criticism in this unique circle of brilliant individuals that the plays of Shakespeare were forged.* It would account for the vast store of varied knowledge in the plays, the immense vocabulary, the polish and repolish of lines.

This would not mean that there were many Shakespeares, but it would mean that the combined wisdom of a group of outstandingly intelligent aristocrats, who met frequently, who had time on their hands, whose greatest relaxation in life was a pursuit of the Muses, who themselves provided an adequate audience and severest critics, led by one master mind, formed a group - a magic circle, without which the divine works of Shakespeare could not have come to their full glory...

It would be reasonable to guess that this Shakespeare group started with *the collaboration of Stanley and Oxford.* Who contributed and how much the various contributions were ultimately worth is probably something which can never be known, but we do know that many of the plays were built on old material, and who can say through what stages they passed or who contributed a touch here and a line there *before they were 'alchemised' into pure gold by the mind of the master.'*

England had been rescued in 1588 by the defeat of the Spanish armada, causing a great surge of national pride. It is credible that a group of highly talented noble persons wanted to write plays that celebrated Englishness - but, without giving their names.[46]

The Author(s)

In Sonnet 81 the poet reflects upon the deal made with Fate whereby he would become the world's greatest playwright *in return for* anonymity, as if the deal stipulated that he could never appear upon the public stage to take the credit, never bask in its glory:

> 'From hence your memory death cannot take / Although in me each part will be forgotten.... Your name from hence immortal life shall have / Though I, once gone, to all the world must die.'

'Your' is (I suggest) here alluding to the corpus of his work ... and not so much to whatever individual is getting the credit for it.

Sonnet 107 describes his creative process. This haunting sonnet alludes to the death of the Queen in 1603:

> Not mine own feares, nor the prophetic soule / Of the wide world dreaming of things to come / Can yet the lease of my true love control / Supposed as forfeit to a confin'd doom. / The mortal moon hath her eclipse endured

'The prophetic soul of the wide world dreaming of things to come' alludes (I suggest) to his muse, the inspiration-process which produced the magnificent tapestries of history unfolding in his plays; while his 'true love' alludes to the creative process, which allowed him to

46 This case is well argued in *Shakespeare's Magic Circle* by AJ Evans, 1956.

compose the immortal works. No-one could 'control' i.e. limit that process - and yet it had been feared that it would all come to an end, 'supposed as forfeit to a confin'd doom,' because the great Queen had died: 'The mortal moon hath her eclipse endured.' Poets would compare her to the moon. Then the good news came that it would not after all end, the new monarch was not so bad:

> And peace proclaims olives of endless age. / Now with the drops of this most balmy time / My love looks fresh....

His plays could still continue! The new king from Scotland promised toleration for different religious views so there would no longer be the awful religious persecutions: 'the drops of this most balmy time' (That religious tolerance, it turned out, hardly lasted for a year). This sonnet tells us how close the Author was to the monarchy. His plays grasped what the English throne was all about – and indeed they did more, they gave to it an immortal glamour.

In his bones, in his blood, he sensed the majesty of that throne and knew how it worked. What is regarded as 'almost certainly' his first play, *Henry the Sixth,* appeared in 1590. One feels the high-level drama of its opening words, cast in 'heroic' iambic-pentameter verse:

> <u>Duke of Bedford:</u> Hung be the heavens with black, yield day to night! / Comets, importing change of times and states, / Brandish your crystal tresses in the sky, / And with them scourge the bad revolting stars / That have consented unto Henry's death! / King Henry the Fifth, too famous to live long! / England ne'er lost a king of so much worth.'

You might not guess from this play that Henry V had died from dysentry aged only 34 and that his son Henry VI succeeded him when just one year old. Thus 'Shakespeare' added glamour and glory to the English throne, which could be why Edward de Vere received a £1000 a year stipend from the Queen. He was rewriting English history to glorify the Elizabethan dynasty, the House of Tudor.

We saw how the plays of 'Shakespeare' opened with a tetralogy of four plays, covering the Wars of the Roses which had torn Britain apart in the fifteenth century: Henry VI parts 1-3 i.e. three plays, followed by *Richard the Third*. What kind of person would start off their career with a quartet of plays displaying a panorama of international history interwoven with the fate of the English crown? One who wished to remain anonymous, for a start! Christopher Marlowe, the greatest playwright around when 'Shakespeare' was first appearing, found himself arrested on a charge of atheism, and may have faked his death to escape the torture-chamber

The ancestors of Edward de Vere, 'Earl of Oxford', had signed the *Magna Carta* with King John and had fought in France with Richard the Lionheart. His family had a proud lineage of warriors and power-brokers. The plays glamorise the de Vere lineage! *Henry VI* alludes to one of his ancestors as 'valiant Oxford' and then as 'brave Oxford, wondrous well belov'd.' That looks like a *reason why* the history-plays started off with three plays about Henry VI, if the de Vere ancestors had participated in the conflicts there described.

Edward could converse fluently in four languages and graduated from the University of Cambridge at the age of only 14.

His father John de Vere the 16th Earl of Oxford had held the lease on the first public theatre, ran his own company of players and was a great patron to the playwrights. The first known historical verse drama in English was *King John* which Queen Elizabeth watched in 1561, acted by John de Vere's company of actors.

Both de Vere and the Earl of Derby had spent time in Italy, which could account for the many comedies of Shakespeare that were based wholly or partly upon Italy:

The Two Gentlemen of Verona, The comedy of Errors, the Taming of the shrew, All's Well that ends Well, The Merchant of Venice, Much Ado about Nothing, Twelfth Night, The Tempest, Winter's Tale and *Romeo and Juliet.*

Thus ten of his fictional plays are set partly or wholly in Italy, whereas only one such is set in England (*the Merry Wives of Windsor*) - a ten-to-one ratio! Thus his plays brought the glory of the Italian Renaissance back to England. De Vere was called 'the Italianate gentleman' upon his return from Italy, on account of his Italian manners and dress. He brought some special gloves for the Queen.

De Vere would wax eloquent about his Italian adventures, and one drinking buddy recalled how he loved to tell a story: 'Diversely hath he told it, and when he enters into it, he can hardly out, which hath made such sport as often have I been driven to rise from his table laughing.'[47]

There he is, the storyteller.

Figure: A portrait of Edward de Vere by a Dutch painter Marcus Gheeraeds c.1586, owned by the Duke of St Albans, a descendant of the de Vere family. Behind the head is written, 'Edward de Vere 17th Earl of Oxford.' Note the rather theatrical style of clothing as one might expect from a play director. He holds the family emblem, a little boar, on a necklace. This is surely the best portrait of him.

Twin souls

Continuing to quote from Evans:

47 Anderson *op. cit.* p.92, quoting Charles Arundel.

Oxford and Derby, already kinsmen and soon to be related by marriage, had in their education, in their lives and in their troubles, quite an astonishing number of similarities and common experiences. Both were scholars and linguists. It is probable that they could converse fluently in four languages, English, French, Italian and Latin. Each had a university education, de Vere at Cambridge and Stanley at Oxford. They both, at different times, studied law at the Inns of Court. Oxford spent over a year abroad, partly in northern Italy, returning to England in 1576 ... Derby went to France in 1582 and remained abroad for several years, travelling widely and spending probably two years or more in Italy before visiting Egypt and the Eastern Mediterranean and possibly joining Leicester in the Netherlands on his way home.

Figure: image of de Vere's son Henry, the 18th Eagrl of Oxford.

Both had great reputations for skill at arms and both fought duels in which they were wounded....Both Derby and Oxford had at different times been patrons of troupes of professional players and both were apparently enthusiastic amateur actors. It is a fact that the professional companies visited the Derby Mansions in Lancashire more frequently during the 1590s than any other house belonging to any of the great nobles....

Figure: William Stanley the 6th Earl of Derby[48]

During the Wars of the Roses the ancestors of both Derby and Oxford had been strong supporters of the House of Lancaster and in the plays Henry VI, Part III, Richard II and Richard III we find that the importance of the roles played by their forebears are emphasised unduly ...For instance in the last scene of Richard III it is Lord Stanley who places the crown on Richmond's head, whilst the other nobles merely stand round in silence. As the Tudors were loyal to the Lancastrian cause it made sense for the Shakespeare plays to favour this side of the conflict.

Both Oxford and Derby, especially the latter, took great interest in magic, astronomy and astrology. Thus the famous Dr John Dee, astrologer to the queen, was Derby's friend and protégé and near

[48] Credit: Bridgeman Images

neighbour in Lancashire, and was also well known to Oxford. Dee, in his diary, notes frequent occasions on which he met Lord Derby or dined with him in Lancashire and London.[49]

The poet John Donne was a friend of the Derby family. He dedicated his 'Holy Sonnets' of c. 1618 to the 'E. of D.' believed to be the Earl of Derby (E.J. Evans, p.99). Donne used an alchemical metaphor:

As fire these drossie Rymes do purifie
Or an elixir, to change them into gold.
You are that alchemist wich always had
Wit, whose one spark could make good things of bad.

It could be a mistake to seek for one or the other as 'the' author.

When William Stanley in 1595 married Elizabeth de Vere, the daughter of Edward de Vere, it is believed that the premier performance of *A Midsummer Night's Dream* was then given. A chronicler recorded,

> The 26th of January, William, Earl of derby, married the earl of Oxford's daughter at the court then at Greenwich, which marriage was there most royally kept.[50]

The play probably received its first performance in the Great chamber of Greenwich Palace on that Sunday night, the 26th. Further wedding celebrations were held north of London at Burghley House in Lincolnshire, culminating at the New Moon of 30th January; echoing the central theme of the play *Midsummer Night's Dream,* where Theseus and Hippolyta are impatiently waiting for the New Moon for their wedding ceremony.

Today, happy couples walk down the aisle to music written by Mendelssohn for the wedding of Theseus and Hippolyta that ends *A Midsummer Night's Dream.*

> Shakespeare was also a truly Renaissance figure in that he loved Courts and Great Houses, where the Renaissance man felt that life could be really lived.[51]

Too much material emerged post-1604 for de Vere to have been the

---

49 *The Diary of John Dee*, pp.52-60
50 John Stow: Anderson, *Shakespeare by Another Name*, p.287.
51 AC Harwood, *Shakespeare's Prophetic Mind,* 1964 p.62.

sole author: 'A very large number of truly Shakespearian alterations and improvements were made in several plays, apparently and, in the case of Richard III certainly after the death of Shakespeare and Oxford' (Evans p154). The last three plays *Cymbeline, The Winter's Tale* and *The Tempest* are believed to date from 1610-11 and they have a different metric structure and a lighter mood – following the great tragedies - with more elements of fairy-tale and the supernatural about them. And, as we've seen, the plays have too many different words for one author. Stanley was made king of the Isle of Man by James in this period, which could in some degree echo the idyllic island in *The Tempest*.

Wonderful fey traditions appear in the later plays, concerning elemental beings -

Ill met by moonlight, proud Titania,

- which could have been more accessible in Wales or the West country of England, than in the streets of London.

Full fathom five thy Father lies
Of his bones are coral made
Nothing of him doth fade
But doth suffer a sea-change
Into something rich and strange

Who wrote that? Surely not someone trained as a lawyer in London? William Stanley would attend the midsummer festivities at Chester, his favourite town and the title *Midsummer Night's Dream* may allude to the midsummer plays that were there produced.[52]

Sonnet 125, 'Were't aught to me I bore the Canopy?' has to allude either to Stanley or de Vere bearing a gold canopy over the Queen in the November 1588 royal procession through London, to celebrate the defeat of the Spanish Armada; or maybe the coronation of King James in 1603, when certain Knights of the Garter had held a 'canopy' above England's new King. It has to have been written by one of them. Stanley

52 Evans (1956, p.57) found 'no doubt' that the name of this play recalled the yearly midsummer plays produced at Chester, and that William Stanley had composed it for his wedding: thus 'Theseus' and 'Hippolyta' in the play were himself and his bride Elizabeth de Vere, while the actors 'Bottom the weaver' etc represented the Chester workmen-actors.

had a better claim to the throne than Elizabeth from his royal lineage, as great-great grandson of Henry VII, Elizabeth having been damned as illegitimate by the Pope. Stanley's line descended directly from Mary Tudor, daughter of Henry VII which meant that he could well be suspected of harbouring Catholic sympathies. In 1594 he became Earl of Derby after which the Queen may well have envisaged him as a possible consort. Some were looking to him as a possible successor to Elizabeth and Catholics favoured him because of his views on religious tolerance. There had been various subversive Catholic plots and in such a milieu he had to take extreme care to preserve the secret of authorship – especially after the shock of his brother 'Lord Strange' having been poisoned in that same year.

W.S. meets W.S.

> 'Most of the great nobles of the Elizabethan age were ardently devoted to poetry and the drama…These troupes toured the country, playing in the big towns an in the great houses of the aristocracy. Indeed private theatricals and frequent visits by the professional players formed a large part in the home amusements of the aristocracy.' (Evans p.39)

In 1587 a troupe of actors performed a lengthy tour across England, stopping at Dover, Canterbury, Oxford, Marlborough, Southampton, Exeter, Bath, Gloucester, *Stratford on Avon, Lathom House Lancaster,* Coventry and Leicester. They stayed at Lord Derby's house at Lathom. By tradition that year or thereabouts is supposed to be the date when Mr Shaxpere left his home town of Stratford. Did he join up with this troupe and thereby arrive at Lord Derby's house? A few months later this troupe came under the patronage of William Stanley's brother, Ferdinando Stanley, known as 'Lord Strange.' That group became known as the Lord Chamberlain's company and was soon acting in the London theatres by the banks of the Thames. Do we not have here some joke whereby William Stanley and William Shaxpere could collude? After all, 'It was impossible for noblemen such as Oxford or Stanley to put plays upon the professional stage in their own names' (Evans, p.44).

The man of Stratford was probably well paid: 'it does seem very possible that Shakspere was doing a job of work for the patron of his company, Lord Strange or his brother William Stanley, and was getting well paid for it.'

Inevitably, the Stratford character started to claim undue credit - one can hardly blame him for this, after all he did have a family to support. Mr Nobody was producing the grand plays one after another, with a name so similar to his own, and was he not acting in some of them? Upon his death in 1616 he received an utterly scornful epitaph from Ben Jonson, published in that year, which began:

Poor Poet-ape, who would be thought our chief,

Whose works are e'en the frippery of wit,

From brokage has become so bold a thief,

As we, the robb'd, leave rage and pity it, etc.

Lord Strange the elder brother of William, dies suddenly aged only 35 in 1594 and 'all the evidence suggested poisoning' such that 'those who gained most from the murder were the Cecils... His death, as events would show, greatly enriched the Cecil family.'[53] He, Ferdinando Stanley, may not have been intending to lead a Catholic rebellion and yet could be viewed as in a position to have done so. Similar comments could be said about the murder of Christopher Marlowe in the previous year, both credibly being black-ops schemed up by Cecil. These tragedies would have exerted a most sobering effect upon William Stanley, indicating that even his ancient, royal house was not safe. They would have rammed home the absolute need for anonymity. for any Author of the plays.

---

53 Clare Asquith, *Shadowplay,the Hidden Beliefs and Coded Politics of William Shakespeare*, 2005, p.90. A scandalous book *A conference about the next succession in the crown of England* was published in 1594, which reckoned Lord Strange was one of the most eligible candidates (Ibid., p81). 'It is no marvel' wrote Sir Richard Yorke in 1594 to William Stanley, 'when Machiavellian policies govern England, I durst pawn my life that the Lord Treasurer caused him to be poisoned that, he being dead, he might marry the young lady Vere unto the brother of the said Earl of Derby.' (p.106)

There seems to be a fairly tight connection between William Stanley and the play *Love's Labours Lost,* which describes in detail events in the French court of Henri of Navarre in 1583 when Stanley was visiting. Reckoned John Michell, Stanley was 'almost certainly' present at the Court of Navarre and the similarities make it 'highly probable' that he was the author. A French author commented on the play: 'It is extraordinary to see how faithfully, even down to the most minute detail, Shakespeare represents historical truth and local colour… in their conversation his ladies and gentlemen are completely French – lively, alert and full of spirit.'[54] In the previous year when Stanley had been in Paris and stayed at the court of Henri III, all of the incidents in *Measure for Measure* took place before his eyes.[55]

THE
MOST LA-
mentable Romaine
Tragedie of Titus Andronicus:
As it was Plaide by the Right Ho-
nourable the Earle of *Darbie*, Earle of *Pembrooke*,
and Earle of *Sussex* their Seruants.

LONDON,
Printed by Iohn Danter, and are
to be sold by *Edward White* & *Thomas Millington*,
at the little North doore of Paules at the
signe of the Gunne,
1594.

<u>Figure:</u> Frontespiece of *Titus Andronicus* published in 1594 'As it was played by the right honourable Earl of Derby' etc., i.e. William Stanley, W.S.!

Thus we are able to appreciate how the fellow from Stratford came to be a part of the story, *provided* we accept that William Stanley had a substantial role in comosing the plays. A troupe of players came to his home, after performing at Stratford-

54 Lefranc, *Sous le Masque de 'William Shakespeare* 1919; Michell, p.200.

55 A.W. Titherley *Shakespeare's Identity* evaluates a handwritten text written by 'Shakespeare,' comprising three pages of a play 'Sir Thomas Moore' written between 1590-1594 (Evans, p. 145). Titherley argued that the handwriting, spelling etc. had to be that of the Earl of Derby: Evans *op.cit.,* Appendix 1.

upon-Avon, and presumably Mr Shaxpere was with them as he then became associated with that group. The Earl of Derby would have made some decision here, which greatly affected the future course of events - perhaps more than he anticipated.

Salon of a Renaissance woman

The lofty subject of heavenly tale
Thames' fairest Swan, our summer's Nightingale.

Michael Drayton on Mary Herbert (*Shepherd's Garland*, 1593)

Mary Herbert known as Lady Pembroke, the sister of Sir Philip Sidney, became in 1577 mistress of Wilton House, located on the banks of Wiltshire's River Avon. 'In her time, Wilton House was like a College, there were so many learned and ingenious persons. She was the greatest Patroness of wit and learning of any lady of her time,' reckoned John Aubrey.[56]

Did she there develop 'the most important literary circle in England's history' (*Sweet Swan of Avon* p.64) and did that become a wonderful centre where Evans' 'Magic Circle' would meet together? Was it indeed, as Evans surmised years ago,

> 'the "home of poetry" and the centre (as I believe) of the "Magic Circle" (ibid, p.69)?

She was, as the historian Adrian Gilbert put it, a true 'Renaissance woman':

> In addition to her academic studies, she learnt how to ride with hounds, hunt with a hawk, shoot with a bow, use a tennis racquet and play the popular game of bowls. As a well-bred woman she was taught poetry and rhetoric from an early age and was expected to learn enough 'Physic' (medicine) as might be needed in due course by the lady of a large household. It went without saying that she

---

56 Aubrey, *Brief Lives*, 'Mary Herbert, Countess of Pembroke (1555-1621): 'This curious seate of Wilton and the adjacent countrey is an Arcadian place and a paradise.'

> learnt how to play the lute and compose melodies of her own. If ever there was a Renaissance woman, it was her!... Mary Sidney now known as the Countess of Pembroke, had been keen on theatre all her life. With her marriage to one of the richest men in the kingdom, she was in a position to become, in the Earl's name, a major patron of the arts. Their home, Wilton House, was at the epicentre of artistic and linguistic revolution. It was probably at Mary's instigation that the Earl sponsored William Shakespeare's company, which was accordingly known as 'Pembroke's Men.' The connection with Shakespeare continued, and when the first folio of his works was published, in 1623, it was dedicated to the 'incomparable pair' the Countess' sons – William Herbert, 3rd Earl of Pembroke, and his brother Philip, Earl of Montgomery and later on 4th Earl of Pembroke. The printing began in February 1621, just weeks after the death of their mother. She, meanwhile, was recently identified in a quite extraordinary book, *Sweet Swan of Avon*, as the real author of Shakespeare's plays…[57]

She must surely be an important part of the story. That brilliant group would meet there in the context of a *new humanism.* Their concern was not primarily religious, the plays were never centred on religion, although perhaps they did in some degree share a hidden and inexpressible love for the religion of old England.[58]

[Thus, the play *Hamlet* is presented within the context of the old religion. Prince Hamlet had the shattering experience of his dead Father returning and claiming to be in Purgatory. Now Purgatory had been wholly abolished by the Protestants: after death you went either to Heaven or Hell, no ifs or buts. And why was Hamlet's poor Father enduring the torments of Purgatory? He was there *because* he had not been shriven by a priest, before dying. This was a rather charming concept of the Catholic church, whereby one would confess anything dire to a priest who would try to forgive it, and he would then give a final blessing, to help improve one's journey into the Great Beyond. But,

57 Adrian Gilbert, *The Blood of Avalon* 2013, p.148.

58 C.f. Thomas Looney's judgement, that he was 'Of probable Catholic leanings, but touched with scepticism' (Ibid., p.103).

that was now totally *verboten* by England's new religion. Towards the end of the play Hamlet cries out, 'angels and ministers of grace defend us.' Again the new religion had forbidden appeal to any such intermediaries, only the Deity itself was to be addressed! So much had been abolished by the new Church of England.]

Only a decade or two earlier, all the plays performed around England had been part of the Mystery cycles structured around Bible stories of the Fall and redemption of man, of Adam and Eve, the Flood etc. The York mystery cycle for example had included thirty speaking parts in its repertoire of fifty plays, each performed by an appropriate craft guild. These had all been abolished in living memory along with so much of old England, while a new and more secular learning was appearing.

The group enjoyed the minting of new words and that *cannot* have been a solitary activity. 'Being a Latin, Greek, Italian and French scholar Mary may well have had some part in swelling the fantastic vocabulary of the plays by anglicising French and Latin words using them as Shakespeare so frequently did in their root meanings. Once that "game" had been started it must have been an irresistible attraction to scholars in the "Circle"' (Evans, p.69). No way could one person have created such a torrent of new phrases, still in use today (See Appendix) – as well as minting so many new words. The Bard is credited with some 1,700 new words.

'We have the man Shakespeare here' wrote Mary Pembroke to her son Philip, urging him to pay a visit.[59] The mind boggles. This was in 1603, as plague was raging in London. The King paid a visit as the play *As you like it* was performed on 2nd of December while Walter Raleigh was loitering in the Tower under a death-sentence, due to be executed on December 9th. Mary had been close to Raleigh and she may have set up the event to work on the King and change his mind – which seems to have worked, as Raleigh was awarded a reprieve.

59 The letter was last seen in 1865, when the poet William Cory recorded it, *Earls of Paradise* p.141.

The first four 'Shakespeare' plays to be published were performed by the 'Pembroke's Men' sponsored by Mary Sidney. The First Folio printing began in April of 1621, then after Mary's death in September the printing stopped in October and did not resume again until November of 1623. Alas there is no-one to tell us what that was all about.

Portrait of William Herbert, 3rd Earl of Pembroke[60]

Her two sons Phillip and William either married or were engaged to de Vere's daughters: which tells us much about who came to own the great manuscript collection. In the early 17th century, William Pembroke had more works dedicated to him than anyone else outside the royal family. He declined to marry various eligible ladies. As 3rd Earl of Pembroke, William would devote his early adulthood to obtaining the particular Court office that gave him control over Shakespeare's company, the King's Men, becoming in 1615 'Lord Chamberlain to the King' which meant that he had the power to push through the publication of the massive text.[61] It was an office he would keep for a decade before passing it on to his younger brother, Philip, Earl of Montgomery, whose first wife was Oxford's youngest daughter. These two are the "peerless brethren" to whom the *First Folio* was dedicated in 1623.

Ben Jonson received a substantial addition to his pension of £100 from William Herbert while he was working in the Pembroke's London

---

60 His statue is in the courtyard of the Bodlean library at Oxford. Pembroke College in Oxford was named after him.

61 Whittemore, F., quoting Eva Turner Clark *Hidden allusions in Shakespeare's Plays* 1974.

home, putting the plays together. The First Folio which eventually came out in 1623 was dedicated to him.

As regards what happened to all of the precious manuscripts which Ben Jonson (it is believed) had been using to prepare the First Folio: his library went up in flames in the year 1623.[62]

An Alter Ego?

De Vere's extant works have a fairly melancholic tone, generally griping about the course of events.[63] Could there have been some alter ego that seized a-hold of him while composing the immortal works? If so, this was powerfully expressed by the learned Stefanie Hughes:

> Shakespeare is not just a pseudonym, purchased by the Lord Chamberlain's Men from William of Stratford so that the plays could be published. Shakespeare the playwright is a being with his own history, an entity as real as Dionysos was to the Greeks or John the Baptist to da Vinci, or Jesus to Christians today. Half human (de Vere), half fiction, Shakespeare (the Poet) had, and still has, a life of his own. He is an immortal that, if anything, was for his creator more like one of the personalities that manifests in people with multiple personality disorder. When de Vere took up his pen, the "spear" that he "shook" in defense of merry-making and platonic love, he was, while engaged in the pursuit of the dramatic truth that he shared with his admired forbears, Euripides, Plautus, and Terence, another, and better, being.[64]

62 Or, if perchance they ended up in the possession of William Stanley the Earl of Derby, his tower at Lathom was burnt down in the Civil War with the loss of family archives.
63 Oxford's verses, 'lack Shakespeare's majestic and flowing rhythm. Moreover there is in them not one spark of real humour or joie de vivre. They are written by an unhappy, frustrated man…' (Evans, Ibid., p.73)
64 Politicworm "did Shakespeare die on 24th of June?"

What follows is a mere personal opinion.[65] Somehow the Bard's *perception* was unrivalled, his ability to *see* what was really happening. Sonnet 33 describes the classic experience of mystic illumination:

Full many a glorious morning have I seen
Flatter the mountain-tops with sovereign eye,
Kissing with golden face the meadows green,
Gilding pale streams with heavenly alchemy;
Anon permit the basest clouds to ride
With ugly rack on his celestial face
And from the forlorn world his visage hide,
Stealing unseen to west with this disgrace.
Even so my sun one early morn did shine
With all-triumphant splendour on my brow;
But out, alack! he was but one hour mine;
The region cloud hath mask'd him from me now.
Yet him for this my love no whit disdaineth;
Suns of the world may stain when heaven's sun staineth.

'Shakespeare' could be describing his creative process in Sonnet 73, as if talking about someone else:

Was it his spirit, by spirits taught to write
Above a mortal pitch, that struck me dead?
No, neither he, nor his compeers by night
Giving him aid, my verse astonished.
He, nor that affable familiar ghost
Which nightly gulls him with intelligence[66]

At night time the stories would come to him, he being taught to write 'above a mortal pitch.' 'That affable, familiar ghost' was probably some old master-alchemist, with a golden touch.

---

65 Or rather, it comes from R.M. Bucke, *Cosmic Consciousness, a study in the evolution of the Human mind,* c.1900. I rather doubt if anyone today (except myself) takes this view.

66 David Roper argued (2018) that Sonnet 86 concerned a rivalry with Raleigh for the Queen's affections, alluding to the 'Ark Raleigh' launched in 1587: 'Was it the proud full sail of his great verse / Bound for the prize of all too precious you'? This alluded, he argued, to Raleigh's circle of occult, night-time studies.

The Bard of the Sonnets is usually viewed as a lame, decrepit old man with one foot in the grave, who doesn't like what he sees in the mirror and is sadly obsessed with a longing for some youth - whose image keeps however changing from sonnet to sonnet. To apprehend how the immortal masterpieces came into being, a less mundane approach may be helpful. Sonnet 53 describes the myriad refracted forms in which his divine vision appears even though it or she somehow retains her unity. So it's a study of unity and multiplicity. The endless variety of characters in his plays were thereby irradiated by gleams from eternity:

> What is your substance, whereof are you made,
> That millions of strange shadows on you tend?
> Since every one hath, every one, one shade,
> And you but one, can every shadow lend.
> Describe Adonis, and the counterfeit
> Is poorly imitated after you;
> On Helen's cheek all art of beauty set,
> And you in Grecian tires [clothes] are painted new:
> Speak of the spring, and foison [harvest] of the year,
> The one doth shadow of your beauty show,
> The other as your bounty doth appear;
> And you in every blessed shape we know.
> In all external grace you have some part,
> But you like none, none you, for constant heart.

That is a mystical vision, of a Presence which irradiates the mundane world and yet is nowhere to be found in it: 'In all external grace you have some part / But you like none, none you, for constant heart.' This vision, which illuminated his life, is connected with classical antiquity, or takes the form of its ideal, however even the beauty of Adonis 'is poorly imitated after you'. He finds her to be a Ceres-like being insofar as comparing her to the spring and autumn, the glory of spring appears as a mere 'shadow' of hers, while the harvest-time of Autumn reminds him of her bounty. She is somehow present 'in every blessed shape we know.' In his plays, the ordinary lead and iron of human existence has become transmuted into imperishable gold and silver. This Sonnet indicates *the process by which* that took place.

A century ago, the Canadian Bucke in his *Cosmic Consciousness* explained this Sonnet by means of a Buddhist text:

> '*Arahatship* [Cosmic consciousness] enables a man to comprehend by his own heart the hearts of other beings and of other men, to understand all minds, the passionate, the calm, the angry, the wise, the concentrated, the ever varying, the lofty, the narrow, the sublime, the mean, the steadfast, the wavering, the free and the enslaved.' That is, it reveals all character, as is so well exemplified in the 'Shakespeare' drama.[67]

That is so, and is how the plays came into being. Those who reckon that this Sonnet is about the Bard pining after some young man – as modern authors seem to agree – have greatly missed the point.

The beginning of Sonnet 14 reminds us of what de Vere would have learnt from studying under the Elizabethan mage, John Dee:

> Not from the stars do I my judgement plucke,
> And yet me thinkes I have Astronomy..

It describes the astrological techniques for forecasting, which the author somewhat decries, or says he will not use, then reaches a wonderful climax concerning whence the Bard does in fact draw his judgement:

> But from thine eyes my knowledge I derive,
> And, constant stars, in them I reach such art
> As truth and beauty shall together thrive

Whose eyes are these? The reader is invited to reflect calmly on this matter. There does not exist a 'right' or correct answer here. From the 'constant stars' in 'thine eyes,' the bard finds himself guided to such a pinnacle of Art, that he is able to find Truth and Beauty *thriving together.* Texts on Sufi mysticism may be helpful here.

The Bard reflects upon how his creations *are immortal:*

Sonnet LV

> Not marble, nor the gilded monuments
> Of princes, shall outlive this powerful rhyme;

---

67 Richard Bucke Ibid., p.144.

But you shall shine more bright in these contents
Than unswept stone, besmear'd with sluttish time.
When wasteful war shall statues overturn…

Gazing into the future, he can know that his Work will outlast even statues of stone - for which he thanks 'you,' i.e. his Muse.

His Muse does now and then desert the Bard, when he can't compose anything! In Sonnet 100 he wonders where She's got to –

Where art thou Muse that thou forget'st so long,
To speak of that which gives thee all thy might?
Spend'st thou thy fury on some worthless song,
Darkening thy power to lend base subjects light?
Return forgetful Muse, and straight redeem,
In gentle numbers [noble verses] time so idly spent;
Sing to the ear that doth thy lays esteem
And gives thy pen both skill and argument.
Rise, resty Muse, my love's sweet face survey,
If Time have any wrinkle graven there;

and implores Her to return, so they can get working again, but also to checkout what he's done: 'my love's sweet face survey' and see if it's flawed in any way: 'If Time have any wrinkle graven there.' As we saw earlier with Sonnet 107, by his 'love' he is here alluding to the creative process, to his Work, to what he loves doing most. The Bard had earlier developed this theme, of his inner desolation during the Muse's absence ('And, thou away, the very birds are mute') in sonnet 97.

Again, if you think this is alluding to some young man, as books will tell you, then you face a couple of problems. Firstly, it in no way aids one in comprehending how the plays came to be written, rather the contrary. Second, *no homosexuals* are depicted in the works of Shakespeare (or if you prefer, no homosexual couples). Yes there is the odd effeminate character, eg Malvolio in *Twelfth Night,* who *might* be gay; or, there again, he might not. So having outrightly homosexual passion, pederasty i.e with a young man - which then, by the way, carried a death penalty - running through the Sonnets hardly matches up with the plays. Somewhat as the Bard depicts no characters smoking tobacco, it just happens that none of his characters are homosexual: or at least, it cannot be shown that any of his characters are homosexual.

Sonnet 77 again expresses gratitude. The secret of his creativity is here being revealed, so we listen carefully:

> So oft have I invoked thee for my Muse
> And found such fair assistance in my verse
> As every alien pen hath got my use [ie followed my example]
> And under thee their poesy disperse.
> Thine eyes that taught the dumb on high to sing…

De Vere in 1591 married the 'court beauty' Elizabeth Trentham, who had formerly been one of the Maids of Honour of the Queen (sadly, no pictures of her remain). A few years later in 1596 the two of them moved into the King's Place in Hackney. Being blissfully bedded with this court beauty may have helped him compose the immortal works, which start emerging after the wedding-date.[68]

Formerly owned by Henry VIII's secretary Thomas Cromwell, King's Place had a classic Tudor long gallery, a private chapel, a Great Hall and a fine courtyard. William Herbert who held its leasehold recorded that it had "a proper lybrayre to laye bokes in" and was "inclosyd on the backside wyth a greate brode dyche and without that a Fayre large garden ... And at the Hither end of the House comynge from London ys a Faire large garden grounde inclosyd with a bricke wall." On moving into this home, the name William Shake-Speare now starts to appear as Author of the plays. While strolling up and down in the garden, his Muse would speak to him.

In the 1590s de Vere disappears from public view and people wonder what has happened.[69] During this 'quiet' period:

> In 1592 he [de Vere] is placed in comfortable circumstances. He is just 42 years of age and therefore entering upon the period of the true maturity of his powers… Then a silence of 12 years .. of comfort and

68 '…we may take the marriage of Edward de Vere with Elizabeth Trentham as synchronizing with the advent of the Shakespearean dramas' – Looney p,.309.

69 'From 1589 onwards the life of Lord Oxford becomes one of mystery' – B.M Ward, op.cit.

> seclusion [which] exactly corresponds to the period of the amazing outpouring of the great Shakespearean dramas..[70]

During this twelve-year period the immortal dramas were published. The phantomic 'Shakespeare' emerges, during this quiet period of de Vere's life. A modern descendent of de Vere was interviewed about how he saw this:[71]

> With Shakespeare you've got a body of work which is entirely mature, there are no juvenilia, no early works. So it's implausible in terms of a human life because you just don't have those inevitable artistic developments, whether stylistic, emotional or whatever. Whereas with Edward de Vere you have the opposite mystery. You have someone (part of whose early poetic corpus we have) who was praised as a playwright by his contemporaries, and as a poet by some of the greatest poets of the time, like Edmund Spenser, and yet we have nothing after 1590. So you've got two half-lives and it's always struck me that when you put those two together they solve each other's mysteries.

They do indeed.

The Queen

The sonnets may well have been published without the Author's knowledge or consent and to be honest, no-one has ever made much sense of them. Scholars tend to agree that "Shakespeare," in the first seventeen of sonnets printed in 1609, was privately urging Southampton to beget a child to continue his bloodline. Would an old man really want to urge a young man to procreate through seventeen sonnets? The idea is absurd whichever way you look at it. Nothing could turn off a young man more than having a father producing sonnets urging him to bang up his daughter! Henry Wriothesley (Southampton) was then being asked to wed Lady Elizabeth de Vere, Cecil's granddaughter. Would this highly eligible bachelor wed de Vere's fifteen-year old daughter? He

70 Thomas Looney, *Shakespeare Identified,* 1920, 2018, p.311; Whittemore, p.260.
71 Charles Beauclerk, founder and President of the de Vere Society, interviewed in its *Newsletter,* July 2022.

too was a 'ward' of Cecil, i.e brought up by Cecil, so legally would have to do what he was told, up to the age of 21 years. He managed to delay things until he was 21, then said no! Good-looking, athletic, rich and a royal favourite, he could afford to be choosy.

Figures: Not compatible? Henry Wriothesley and Elizabeth de Vere.

Could any of the sonnets have been addressed to the Queen, urging her to procreate? We're told that, in the year 1569 when Oxford was a mere youngster of nineteen years:

> 'My Lord Oxford is lately grown into great credit, for the queen's majesty delighteth more in his presence and his dancing and valiantness, than any other .. At all these love matters my Lord Treasurer winketh, and will not meddle in any way.' (Cecil was the Lord Treasurer.)[72]

72 Letter of Gilbert Talbot to his father the Earl of Shrewsbury: Dorothy and Charlton Ogburn *This Star of England* sourcetext.com/chapter-5/.

Was it not that love which brought forth the great creations, celebrated in the royal performances? The Queen in 1585 signed an extraordinary warrant for de Vere to be given £1000 every year and that was renewed by King James. De Vere's biographer Ward enquired as to what this was for, after all de Vere 'did none of the things we might have expected. He did not serve her as a Minister, as a Privy Councillor, as an Ambassador or as a soldier.' Ward concluded that it was because 'He was instrumental... in providing the court with dramatic entertainment.' (p.282, Ward) Some of the Sonnets, we don't know how many, would have been addressed to her. One motive for composing the plays was, to entertain the Queen.

Let's make a cautious statement about the identity of the Bard: *the perceived catastrophe of a terminating dynasty, i.e. of Elizabeth producing no heirs, echoed deeply in his soul.*

'My early sonnets all reminded Eliza of what she knew well but ever sought to avoid, the solemn duty laid upon Her by Her Father and Her council of ministers, to which had recently been added the clamorous voice of Parliament, to produce an heire for England.'

Queen Elizabeth in 1575

– that, in a semi-fictional biography, is imagined to be de Vere's statement.[73] De Vere would then have been very young. Some take the view that there was a child of Queen Elizabeth, a secret child, the matter of these sonnets: 'Oxford/Shakespeare's appeal to the Fair Youth to marry and sire children, therefore, was an appeal for the survival of the Tudor dynasty.' Concerning the symbolism used

73 Andrew Field, *The lost chronicle of Edward de Vere*, 1990, p199.

throughout the Sonnets, '"Beauty" and "Beauty's Rose" were words directly applied to Queen Elizabeth by other authors multiple times.'[74]

We reflect upon the opening words of the first Sonnet with this in mind:

From fairest creatures we desire increase
That thereby beauty's rose might never die

Does this express a hope that the Tudor dynasty of England might not end – or, does it merely urge the Earl of Southampton to impregnate someone? If the latter it would be most impertinent. Many an ode to the queen commented upon her eyes, of something special about her gaze, as in this Sonnet:

But thou, contracted to thine own bright eyes,
Feedst thy light's flame with self-substantial fuel

It concerns a woman who is admired by the world and is unique, there being only one of her:

Thou that art now the world's fresh ornament
And only herald to the gaudy spring

The fourth Sonnet continues urging the monarch to procreate:

Unthrifty loveliness, why dost thou spend
Upon thy self thy beauty's legacy?

And ends:

For having traffic with thy self alone,
Thou of thy self thy sweet self dost deceive:
Then how when nature calls thee to be gone,
What acceptable audit canst thou leave?
Thy unused beauty must be tombed with thee,
Which, used, lives th' executor to be.

---

74 Kastherine Chiljan, 'Why was Edward de Vere Defamed on stage – and his death Unnoticed?' in *The Oxfordian*, Vol 21, 2019, p.30.

Nobody writes to a man like that! It has to be addressed to a woman, about the danger of remaining childless. Why would anyone want to do that? They would do that because, she's the Queen of England.

The fifth Sonnet begins,

> Those hours, that with gentle work did frame
> The lovely gaze where every eye doth dwell

On whose lovely gaze does every eye dwell? Surely, according to the poets and courtiers, it was that of their 'Virgin Queen'. No-one but de Vere was close enough to her to get away with writing such personal messages: readers may wish to peruse the opening sequence of Sonnets, if perchance we have here clarified their subject-matter, and note how one can enjoy reading them for the first time. For example, Sonnet number seven starts off about the experience of courtly music which the queen loved, then subtly segues into the joys of family life and the need to create one. Would anyone address that to a man?

An implication here, is that these early Sonnets must have been composed decades prior to publication. The great hope failed of course, and the Tudor dynasty of England came to an end in 1603, with De Vere dying a year later.

A later sonnet alludes to rivalry between the Bard and Walter Raleigh, for the Queen's affections, as credibly interpreted by David Roper:[75]

> O! how I faint when I of you do write,
> Knowing a better spirit doth use your name,
> And in the praise thereof spends all his might,
> To make me tongue-tied speaking of your fame.
> But since your worth, wide as the ocean is,
> The humble as the proudest sail doth bear,
> My saucy bark, inferior far to his,
> On your broad main doth wilfully appear.
> Your shallowest help will hold me up afloat,
> Whilst he upon your soundless deep doth ride;

75 David Roper, *How Science proved Edward de Vere was Shakespeare*, 2018 Ch. 10.

Or, being wracked, I am a worthless boat,
He of tall building, and of goodly pride:
  Then if he thrive and I be cast away,
  The worst was this, my love was my decay.

Raleigh had been composing poems of adulation for the Queen, and the Bard here feels some competition. He alludes to the large ship the *Ark Raleigh* launched in 1587, as compared to his much smaller ship the *Edward Bonaventure* that was alas wrecked off the coast of Bermuda: 'my saucy bark, inferior far to his.' Raleigh's great ocean voyages are alluded to, 'While he upon your soundless deep doth ride,' as is also the tall tower of his ancestral home, 'He of tall building' and to his haughty and proud manner on which everyone remarked: 'and of goodly pride.' This may help us to focus upon the Bard's position at court, as a royal favourite. Raleigh's fall from grace came when he impregnated one of the queen's Maids of Waiting - strictly forbidden as they were meant to be chaste – for which he was clapped in the Tower for a few months.

The Earl of Essex

Our interpretation of the opening Sonnets ('From fairest creatures we desire increase') views them as meditations upon the succession of the Crown of England. As such they have to have been addressed to the Queen (page 56) and that would make sense only if she had had one (or possibly more) illegitimate children. De Vere was known not to have favoured the Scottish king as heir to the throne, which got him into some trouble after Eliza's death in 1603.

If so, if she had such a child, then the Robert Deveraux the 2nd Earl of Essex would seem to be the odds-on favourite. See eg the acclaimed film *Anonymous* about de Vere as Shakespeare. The one thing Essex had urgently wanted, upon returning from his failed Irish expedition in 1601, was a private hearing with the Queen, being convinced he could then explain everything. That is why Cecil was so determined to prevent it, and to have him arrested and tried instead. The liberties which Essex had taken in Ireland – not quite following orders which the queen had given him – and his conviction that he could justify himself if only he were allowed an audience with the Queen – would make sense on this basis. Essex was hoping to gain the position of chief advisor to the queen, in place of Cecil: which would have made England a different place. Essex was much loved by the people while Cecil was, generally, hated. After the execution of Essex the queen lost much of her popularity and she sunk into an inconsolable depression.

Digressing slightly, it may be inadvisable to believe that de Vere was having sex with the Queen as highly esteemed sources such as Mark Anderson and Hank Whittemore have accepted, and featuring in the film *Anonymous.* Apart from her being nearly twenty years older than him, an affair with the Queen would create dire complications for him. It was I suggest the most intense, profound and longest-lasting relationship in his life, featuring in his jousting tournaments and in many of the plays, but was more in the nature of *agape* rather than *eros* if one may use the Greek words. She flirted with him surely, but it may be advisable to accept the view of the imaginary de Vere autobiography by Field, that:

> Of all the courtiers around Her, I was the only one who was not at her disposal, though I fear She often mistook my natural manners and jousting for signs of more than they were.[76]

John Dee

John Dee, the last royal wizard, was jailed for casting royal horoscopes of the Queen and her sister. His defence was, that they asked him to do it! But, to seek to divine, by any unlawful means, what a monarch might do in the future was strictly forbidden. In Dee's list of those who supported him during the trial, we read: 'the honourable the Earl of Oxford, his favourable letters, anno 1570.' The twenty-year old de Vere was about to become the highest ranking earl at the court of Elizabeth. 'We may conjecture that it was in 1570 that Oxford studied

---

[76] Andrew Field, *Lost chronicles of Edward de Vere* 1990 p.144.

astrology under Dr Dee.[77] We shall meet these two again later, working together as 'adventurers' attempting to find a North-West passage to China and the east Indies.' (hankwhittemore.com, 'John Dee + Prospero') It is a wonderful image, of 'the man who was Shakespeare' being taught by that learned mage: and could throw a whole new light upon *The Tempest,* one of his final plays if not the final one. Dee signed his letters to Queen Elizabeth with the secret code number '007' and coined the phrase, 'the British Empire.'

Consider –

For who marketh better than he
The seven turning flames of the sky?
Or hath read more of the antique.
Hath greater knowledge of the tongues:
Or understands sooner the sounds
Of the learner to love music?

Is that Prospero, or do the first three lines sound like Dee? It was in fact addressed to the Edward de Vere: "In 1584 a Frenchman and member of Oxford's household, John Southern, dedicated to the Earl a pamphlet of poems entitled *Pandora.* His tribute asserted that Oxford's knowledge of the "seven turning flames of the sky" (the sun, moon and the visible planets, through astrology) was unrivalled; that his reading of "the antique" (a noun referring to classical and ancient history) was unsurpassed; that he had "greater knowledge" of "the tongues" (languages) than anyone; and that his understanding of "sounds" that helped lead students to the love of music was "sooner" (quicker) than anyone else's."[78]

It has to be the Bard himself, here addressed.

An argument advocating William Stanley as the Author was given by William Titherley. Sonnet 135 does after all twice state, 'my name is Will,' which is how Stanley referred to himself. Titherley reckoned that:

> 'While other playwrights occasionally made dramatic use of astrology and magic, with Shakespeare they so permeate his entire

77 Ward 17th Earl of Oxford, p.49
78 hankwhittemore.com/ Dee - Prospero

> work in constant and subtle images, as to show that he had not only meditated profoundly on these mysteries but on the whole riddle of the heavens… this intense fascination which all the occult arts had for Shakespeare was part and parcel of Stanley's immense erudition.'79

No monarch was ever more opposed to magic and witchcraft than James – after all, did he not publish the new Bible with the terrible words 'You shall not suffer a witch to live' which did so much to kindle the witch-burning craze of the 17th-century? Who could be so assured as to dare present *The Tempest,* with its final image of the serene mage, before the king? Prospero did renounce his magic in the end, when leaving the enchanted island. Some reckon this must have been composed by Stanley, after all de Vere was really dead by then, wasn't he?

That play was performed at the marriage of King James' daughter Elizabeth to the emperor Frederick who was to become king of Bohemia, over the Christmas period of 1612/13. And yet – as John Dee was out of favour with the new Stuart monarch - likewise what is regarded as 'Shakespeare's last play' *The Tempest* could never be published on its own, maybe because its themes of magic and enchantment were unduly disapproved of by the King.

The Three Sisters

> *'Susan de Vere was clearly a beautiful and entrancing woman. Ben Jonson fell in love with her and wrote her the most subtly erotic poems…"*[80]

Ben Jonson's wrote a poem to Susan de Vere, Countess of Montgomery:[81]

> Were they that named you, prophets? Did they see
> Even in the dew of grace, what you would be?
> Or because some scarce think that story true,
> To make those faithful did the Fates send you.
> Were you advanced, past those times to be,

---

79 Titherley, W., *Shakespeare's Identity* 1952, p.39

80 Nicholson, A. *Earls of Paradise, England and the Dream of perfection,* 2008, p.180.

81 H. Friedberg, 'Ben Jonson's poetry' Vol. 4, No. 1, *Studies in Renaissance Poetry* (Winter 1974), pp. 111-136.

The light and mark unto posterity?

Was Susan de Vere the 'grand possessor' & producer of the first folio? She appears in more of Jonson's masques than anyone else and his 'Mask of Blackness' was dedicated to her. The publishing house of William Jaggard had brought out four editions of Bacon's *Essays,* then in 1619 produced a compendious opus *Archaeo Ploutos* (of which I cannot find any copy) with a dedication rather similar to the 2023 First folio: 'to the most Noble and Twin-like paire,' only this time its Sir Philip Herbert and his wife Susan de Vere. Now Philip Herbert did have a reputation - quite the opposite of his learned brother - that he 'pretended to no other qualifications than to understand horses and dogs very well' and 'did not delight in books or poetry'[82] – i.e., he was just Susan's rather thick husband. But he cut a fine, sportsmanlike image at the Court. The wonderful awards the King had conferred upon him - Knight of the Bath and Earle of Montgomery - were a result of favours he had done as a good-looking young man to the homosexual king: before he married Susan, one should hasten to add.

Who had the texts? In 1609 a 'Shakespeare' play was published – (*Troilus and Cressida*) which alluded in a preface to the 'Grand Possessors' – the publisher had managed to wrest it from the clutches of the 'Grand Possessors.' Baconians reckon that Francis Bacon owned them, owing to their greatly mistaken belief that he was their Author; while Evans reckoned back in the 1950s that 'The person most likely to have been, what we would now call, the honourable secretary of the Shakespeare society was Mary, Lady Pembroke, Sir Philip Sidney's sister' (p.68).

The dedication of the 1619 opus was thus 'to the truly virtuous and Noble Countess his Wife, the Lady Susan, Daughter to the right Honourable Edward de Vere, Earle of Oxford, Viscount ... and lord High Chamberlain of England, etc.' The publisher Jaggard added as a sales blurb:

---

82 Clarendon, History of the Rebellion and Civil wars in England, 1, page 74; 2nd quote John Aubrey.

> …the dedication itself invites both patrons to "enter into a spacious Forrest"–evidently a metaphor for the world of historical customs embodied in *ARXAIO-PLOUTOS* – "affording all choise of pleasing Game, either for Hawking, Hunting, Fishing, Fowling, or any other Noble exercise beside."

He went on to assure his patrons that,

> "…an Orchard stands wide open to welcome you, richly abounding in the fairest Frutages: not to feed the eie only, but likewise to refresh the Heart, inviting you to plucke where, and while you please, and to bestow how, and when you list: because

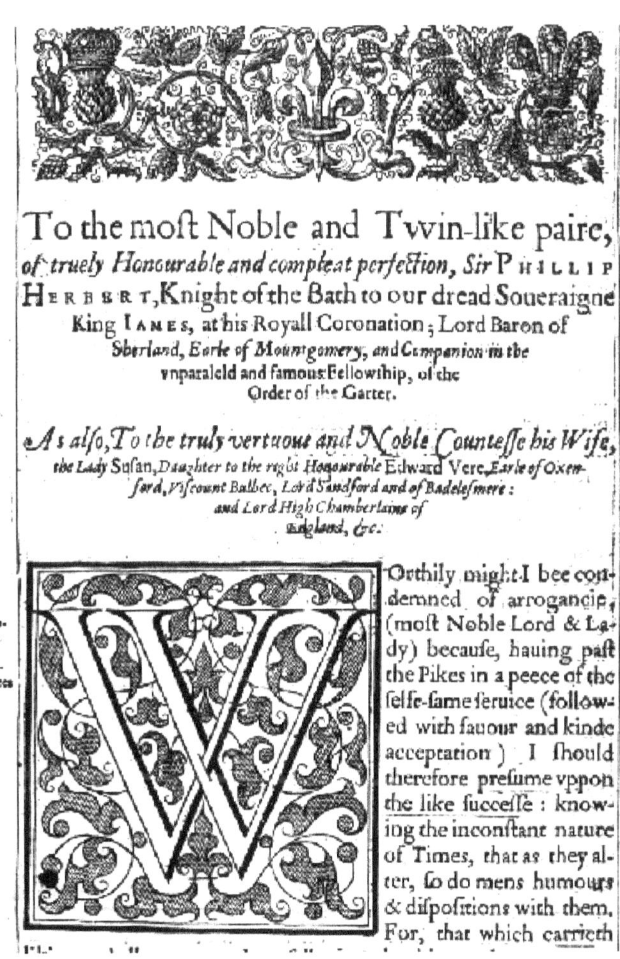

To the most Noble and Twin-like paire, *of truely Honourable and compleat perfection, Sir* PHILLIP HERBERT, Knight of the Bath to our dread Soueraigne King IAMES, at his Royall Coronation; Lord Baron of *Sherland, Earle of Mountgomery, and Companion in the* vnparaleld and famous Fellowship, of the Order of the Garter.

As also, To the truly vertuous and Noble Countesse his Wife, the Lady Susan, *Daughter to the right Honourable* Edward Vere, *Earle of Oxenford, Viscount Balbec, Lord Sandford and of Badelesmere: and Lord High Chamberlaine of England, &c.*

WOrthily might I bee condemned of arrogancie, (most Noble Lord & Lady) because, hauing past the Pikes in a peece of the selfe-same seruice (followed with fauour and kinde acceptation) I should therefore presume vppon the like successe: knowing the inconstant nature of Times, that as they alter, so do mens humours & dispositions with them. For, that which carrieth they are all yours, and whosoever else shall taste of them, do enioy such freedome but by your favor."

Figure: Dedication of *ARXAIO-PLOUTOS* in 1619 to Sir Philip Herbert and his wife Lady Susan de Vere, published by Jaggard and Sons.

In this garden, Jaggard assures Lady Vere,

> ...you may meete with a faire Bevey of Queenes and Ladies, at diverse turnings as you walke, and everie one will tell you the Historie of her life and fortune (rare examples of Vertue and Honor) as themselves can best, truly & plainly discourse unto you. Some other also you shall see, sadly sitting under Eughe & Cipresse tress, with Garlands of those leaves wreathed about their heads, sighing out their divers disasters: whom your noble nature cannot choose but commiserate; as greeving to see a scratch in a cleare skin, and a bodie beautified by Nature, to be blemished by unkinde Destiny.
>
> 'Is Jaggard, in this final passage, referring to the bounteous literary exploration of female experience embodied in the "Shakespeare" canon? Certainly, his language calls to mind characters such as Ophelia, Desdemona, Cleopatra, Lucrece or Imogen –who all are made to tell "the history" of their "lives and fortunes" in a manner quite unprecedented for early 17th century England and undoubtedly quite capable of stirring considerable emotional response in a cultivated arts patron such as Lady Vere. She was one who could commiserate with the "divers disasters" of such characters, not only from literary precedent, but out of secret sympathy with her own father and other relatives who had survived the hurricane of his life.'[83]

Jaggard is saying that his patrons are stewards of the orchard: the fruits "are all yours, and whosoever else shall taste of them, do enioy such freedome but by your favor." These stewards are therefore urged to

---

83 Stritmatter, R. 'Susan de Vere, William Jaggard and the 1623 Shakespeare Folio' *Shakespeare Oxford Newsletter*, Fall 1998.

"...bestow how, and when you list [i.e., please]." That sounds very much as if he has seen the contents of the First Folio and is angling for permission to publish.

The Jaggard publishing house was trying to reach out to and impress 'the lady Susan,' she being the one who has to agree for them to get the big prize viz. publishing the First Folio a couple of years later. This opus dedicated to Susan de Vere and her husband would seem to be targeting them, for access to the Herberts' possession of the unpublished 'Shakespeare' manuscripts.[84]

Dedication of the First Folio

Only three men received dedications of Shakespeare works. Each man had been engaged to (or was married to) one of Oxford's daughters

Earl of Southampton engaged to Elizabeth de Vere
She married William Stanley, 6th Earl of Derby

William Herbert, Earl of Pembroke, engaged to Bridget de Vere

Philip Herbert, Earl of Montgomery, married Susan de Vere

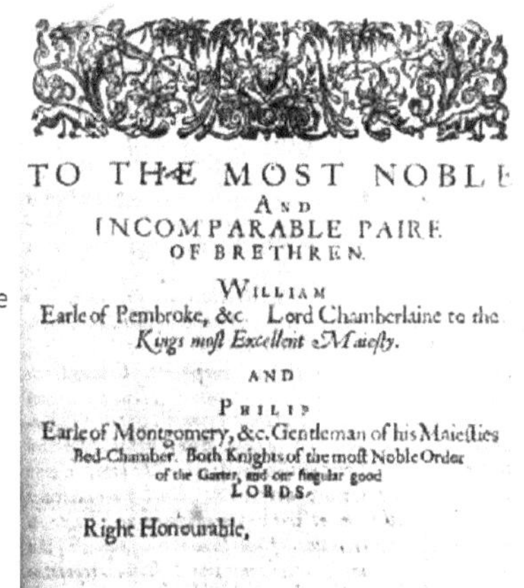

TO THE MOST NOBLE
AND
INCOMPARABLE PAIRE
OF BRETHREN.
WILLIAM
Earle of Pembroke, &c. Lord Chamberlaine to the Kings most Excellent Maiesty.
AND
PHILIP
Earle of Montgomery, &c. Gentleman of his Maiesties Bed-Chamber. Both Knights of the most Noble Order of the Garter, and our singular good
LORDS.
Right Honourable,

We've seen how that First Folio with its nine hundred pages was dedicated to two brothers: William Herbert, Earl of Pembroke (engaged in 1597 to Oxford's second daughter, Bridget de Vere) and Philip Herbert, Earl of Montgomery (who married Oxford's youngest daughter, Susan de Vere, in 1604). Thus the publication of the Shakespeare folio appears as "a family affair" - which began with the marriage of Susan de Vere and Philip Herbert during the 1604-05 Christmas season, at the court of King James, six months after Oxford's reported death on 24 June 1604. Court festivities for the wedding included performances of seven "Shakespeare" plays, clearly a tribute to the absent author.

84 Johnston, Ibid The Oxfordian 2019 (21), p.80.

The Court held the first-ever *Shakespeare-fest* with these performances, a tribute to the memory of de Vere. It began with "The Moor of Venice" (*Othello*) and *The Merry Wives of Windsor* then two more were performed, before and after the main event in 1604:

on 26 December, *Measure for Measure*;

on 27 December the Wedding of Susan de Vere and Philip Herbert,

on 28 December *The Comedy of Errors.*

In January the performances continued with *Love's Labour's Lost*, hosted by Southampton, followed *by Henry the Fifth* and *The Merchant of Venice.*

A masque by Ben Jonson was also acted, where its performers included the bride and groom, Susan and Philip as well as Elizabeth de Vere and her husband, Derby; plus Bridget de Vere's former fiancé William Herbert, Earl of Pembroke. That family remained close to Ben Jonson - a long and intimate association between the daughters of the Earl of Oxford and their families and Ben Jonson - which climaxed in 1623 with the publication of the First Folio. Jonson remained "particularly close" to Susan de Vere and the Herbert brothers, Pembroke and Montgomery, with Pembroke bestowing on Jonson a sizeable stipend every New Year; whereby he was commissioned to collaborate with Francis Bacon in having the great works made presentable and ready to publish.

In summary:

> The collection of Shakespeare's plays published in 1623, the First Folio, gives every appearance of being the fruit of 20 years of association among Ben Jonson, the three de Vere daughters, Elizabeth, Bridget and Susan, and the Herbert brothers, William 3rd Earl of Pembroke, and Philip, 1st Earl of Montgomery.[85]

[85] Ramón Jiménez 'the Case for Oxford Revisited,' *The Oxfordian* 2009, XI, reprinted in the de Vere Society Newsletter, October 2021, p.31.

Part 3: The Man Who was Hamlet

The Play as Autobiography

A whole new interest in the play *Hamlet* can develop, once its autobiographical character is appreciated. We may start with Hamlet giving stage-directions to a group of players. The reader may wish to turn back to the portrait of de Vere on page 37, and dwell on it while mulling over the following lines: does it not show someone who has spent a lifetime in the theatre? And are these lines not, by the way, the best advice ever given to an actor?

HAMLET: Speak the speech, I pray you, as I pronounced it to you, trippingly on the tongue. But if you mouth it, as many of our players do, I had as lief the town crier spoke my lines. Nor do not saw the air too much with your hand, thus, but use all gently, for in the very torrent, tempest, and (as I may say) whirlwind of your passion, you must acquire and beget a temperance that may give it smoothness.

O, it offends me to the soul to hear a robustious periwig-pated fellow tear a passion to tatters, to very rags, to split the ears of the groundlings, who for the most part are capable of nothing but inexplicable dumb shows and noise. I would have such a fellow whipped for o'erdoing Termagant. It out-herods Herod. Pray you avoid it. Be not too tame neither, but let your own discretion be your tutor. Suit the action to the word, the word to the action, with this special observance, that you o'erstep not the modesty of nature. For anything so overdone is from the purpose of playing, whose end, both at the first and now, was and is, to hold, as 'twere, the mirror up to nature, to show virtue her own feature, scorn her own image, and the

> very age and body of the time his form and pressure. Now this overdone, or come tardy off, though it make the unskillful laugh, cannot but make the judicious grieve, the censure of the which one must in your allowance o'erweigh a whole theatre of others.
>
> O, there be players that I have seen play, and heard others praise, and that highly (not to speak profanely), that neither having th' accent of Christians, nor the gait of Christian, pagan, nor man, have so strutted and bellowed that I have thought some of Nature's journeymen had made men, and not made them well, they imitated humanity so abominably. Reform it altogether! And let those that play your clowns speak no more than is set down for them, for there be of them that will themselves laugh, to set on some quantity of barren spectators to laugh too, though in the meantime some necessary question of the play be then to be considered. That's villainous and shows a most pitiful ambition in the fool that uses it. Go make you ready.

We are impressed by the way in which Hamlet is accustomed to managing and directing an acting company. Likewise, De Vere had his own acting company as did his father before him. He was no prince as was Hamlet, however there were no princes in the court of Elizabeth and de Vere was the nearest thing to it, being the highest-ranking earl in the country. When Hamlet welcomes the players –

> You are welcome, masters! Welcome all! - I am glad to see thee well – Welcome good friends – O, old friend! ... Masters, you are all welcome! We'll e'en to't like French falconers, fly at anything we see. We'll have a speech straight. Come give us a taste of your quality, come a passionate speech! (2.2)

we sense that acting was in de Vere's blood and in his bones. So too is falconry - how casually does the comparison with falconry appear! One even notes a disparaging comment against the French, who were allegedly unable to control their falcons, so they would 'fly at anything.' The world has imagined for centuries that the Bard was one of the actors, but how wrong that was: the experience here is that of the manager, welcoming his employees. The Bard is the boss. The above quote by

Hamlet also hints at the interactive process whereby the plays came to be written in the first place.

Lord Willoughby, married to de Vere's sister lady Mary Vere, was sent by Queen Elizabeth in 1582 to the castle at Elsinore in Denmark on a diplomatic mission, Denmark having become one of the great powers of Europe under the reign of king Frederick II. De Vere would have heard all about it at dinner parties with his sister. Lord Willoughby later wrote up his visit, telling how he had got on well with the monarch and recalling his good times there.[86] Cannons would be fired off during the drinking sessions! As the King in the play remarked, 'No jocund health that Denmark drinks today, but the great canon in the clouds shall tell…' (1,2) Hamlet had scruples about this tradition:

> This heavy-headed revel east and west / Makes us traduc'd and tax'd of other nations / They clip us drunkards… (Act 1,Scene 4)

The play begins with the death of Hamlet's father and his replacement at court by one whom Hamlet does not like. De Vere's father died when he was merely twelve years old and he was therefore brought up as the Ward of Robert Cecil, the Queen's Secretary of State. His mother quickly married another considerably below her status, which again happens in this play.

Details of the 'ghost's platform' at Elsinore castle were corrected from King James' Ambassador's visit there in 1603.

Next the scene shifts to Ophelia, receiving advice from her brother Laertes, then some more from her father, Polonius. The former's advice is well-meant, about how she should be careful of offering her affections to Hamlet as he is a royal prince; however the latter is just her father interfering in what is not his business, even manging to get his hands on Hamlet's love-letters to his daughter. Quizzing her in detail about her relationship to Hamlet, Polonius scoffs at any notion of true love and tells her not to be so naïve – all of which basically kills the relationship. Ophelia is too dependent upon her interfering and nosey father to be

86 Whittemore, p.30;Anderson, p.191.

capable of having a relationship with anyone. She is thus portrayed as quite a weak character. Then later on she appears as genuinely bewildered and heartbroken as to why Hamlet does not love her any more. What have I done, she asks him? Hamlet senses that Polonius is too close to her, for this relationship to be feasible. Ditto for Anne Cecil to de Vere, asking the same bewildered question. The play mirrors the enigma of why de Vere would not speak to his wife Anne for several years. She too had grown up as a Ward of Court in the same household on the Strand, Cecil's mansion. The young De Vere did *not* choose her, he was pressured into the marriage by Cecil and the Queen.[87] He seems not to have received the wedding-dowry from Cecil as would have helped his troubled finances.

As his son Laertes is about to depart for France, Polonius gives him the famous precepts on how to live. Scholars have for long agreed, that these derive from the precepts of Lord Burghley, William Cecil, published after his death in 1613, intended for his son Robert and given to him in 1584 before he departed to France. There can be no doubt of the analogy here presented, whereby the Bard has greatly improved upon the advice given by the Queen's Secretary of State to his son and then later published.[88] That in turn implies that he must have been in a position to peruse them before publication, as de Vere clearly was, having grown up in the Cecil household.

Such parallel family structures had been noticed by commentators long before the current authorship debates got going: between Queen Elizabeth, her celebrated Lord High Treasurer William Cecil, his second son Robert and daughter Anne and in the *Hamlet* play: as likewise the close similarity of the 'Certain Precepts' which Burghley wrote out for his son with those given by Polonius.

---

87 'The Earl of Oxford hath gotten him a wife – or at the least a wife hath caught him; this is mistress Anne Cecil' -letter by Lord St John Rutland to the Earl of Rutland, Ward p. 61.
88 William Cecil, Lord Burghley, was the Queen's Secretary of State from 1557 to 1572, then Lord treasurer from 1572 to 1598,

Burghley	Polonius
Be not scurrilous in conversation, or satirical in thy jests	Give thy thoughts no tongue, nor any un-proportioned thought his act … be thou familiar, but by no means vulgar
Neither borrow of a neighbour or friend, but of a stranger, whose paying for it thou shalt hear no more of it… Trust not any man with thy life credit or state.	Neither a borrower nor a lender be, for loan oft loses both itself and friend, and borrowing dulls the edge of husbandry.
Let thy kindred and allies be welcome at thy house and table. Grace them with thy countenance… But shake off those glow-worms, p25	Those friends thou hast, and their adoption tried, grapple them to thy soul with hoops of steel; but do nor dull thy palm with entertainment of each newly-hatched unfledged comrade

That fast approaches a cast-iron proof of authorship.

Once Cecil's son Robert was in Paris, his father's spies started reporting back about his 'inordinate love of .. dice and cards'.[89] Likewise Polonius in the play instructs Reynaldo to ascertain how his lazy son Laertes is enjoying his life, and whether he is 'drinking, fencing, swearing, quarrelling or falling out at tennis.'

'Falling out at tennis' is not a very common phrase and one imagines it would not be easy to do. But, it notably happened to De Vere, indeed it's the only thing most people have heard about him: how he had a spat with Sir Philip Sidney where he 'pulled rank' and Sidney supposedly had to leave the tennis court.

Polonius discusses with Ophelia the reason for Hamlet's distant behaviour, wondering, could it be that they two are mere commoners, not having noble blood? De Vere was troubled by this, and Robert Cecil

89 *The Oxfordian,* 21, 2019: Bruce Johnson, *What role did the Herbert family play in the Shakespeare cover-up?* pp.65-94, 79.

managed to get himself promoted to Lord Burghley in 1571, the year in which the 21-year old de Vere married his daughter, to try and mitigate this problem. So he married the *Countess* Anne Cecil.

Polonius protests to the Queen about Hamlet's behavior: 'Tell him his pranks have been too broad to bear with, and that your Grace hath screened and stood between much heat and him' (3,4). Authorship of the plays had to be hid, because their stories touched so closely the English crown. Elizabeth loved the sometimes shocking manner in which de Vere placed court characters into the plays, and sensed how she was oftentimes depicted therein, whereas Robert Cecil did not, we may suppose, appreciate the way in which the evil hunchback Richard III was portrayed, in which everyone could see an expression of his wily ways. Incisive political comment went into the plays, whereby any other author would have lost their head. Thereby the Mystery developed, of the unknown Author.

As a prank 'too broad to bear with' one may consider the shocking way in which de Vere's servants sprung upon Treasury agents on the Gad's Hill road on the way to Gravesend in 1573. The two men accosted - formerly employees of de Vere - were travelling on state business for William Cecil the Lord Treasurer, carrying money intended for the exchequer. Was de Vere then employing highway robbers? They seem to have been emulating an act which the young Prince Hal (due to become Henry IV) and some comrades had actually done - in the same place, the highway near Gad's Hill, where the money had been intended for the exchequer (Whittemore, p.45). Later on the drama was to appear in the play Henry IV Part 1 with the character of Falstaff included.[90] The Lord Treasurer's men submitted a complaint to Cecil about the attack: 'three of my Lord of Oxford's men ... who lay privily in a ditch awaiting our coming with full intent to murder us...' - the three were duly imprisoned. It was recorded of the young Henry IV that he and companions would indeed lay in wait like highway robbers for an ambush, however afterwards if complaint was made he would return

90 Anderson p.66.

the stolen funds and treat it all as a prank, adding a further reward to the distressed gentlemen. There was an early play *The Famous Victories of Henry the Fifth* performed during the 1580s, thought to be by de Vere, because most of its contents ended up in the Shakespeare plays about Henry IV and V. It looks like being a very early, youthful 'Shakespeare' play of which we have the text, possibly composed in 1574 following the robbery-ambush by de Vere and his men. If the 'youthful prank' of Prince Hal in *Henry IV* was historical, then why was it emulated by de Vere's employees?[91] At some level the answer has to be, that the artist needs to experience the scene if he is later to re-enact it. If you wish to enjoy the play then you have to forgive what he did! Nonetheless one may agree with Polonius that here, "his pranks have been too broad to bear with."

The story moves through four different levels: the original escapade by the young prince Henry, de Vere's rerun using his household employees, the very early 'Shakespeare' play *the Famous Victories of Henry IV*, then finally *Henry IV Part 1* which appears in 1599. That play featured the Boars' Head Tavern in Eastcheap, forever associated with the character of Falstaff and his merry scenes with Prince Hal: "In 1602 the Lords of the Council gave permission for the servants of the Earls of Oxford and Worcester to play at the Tavern", viz. that same Boar's Head.[92]

Queen Elizabeth's father murdered her mother, so she probably enjoyed the dire nemesis which unfolds through *Hamlet*. A strange torment afflicts the phantom figure of Hamlet's Father: 'My hour is almost come / When I to sulphurous and tormenting flames / Must render up myself,' while spending his allotted span in purgatory. De Vere announced his Catholicism upon returning from Italy in 1576.

While returning home from Italy, de Vere's ship was accosted by pirates and ransacked. The French ambassador reported that de Vere had been 'left naked, stripped to his shirt, treated miserably… and that

91 Whittemore pp,45-7.

92 Whittemore p.377, citing Halliwell-Phillips *Outlines of the Life of Shakespeare1883.*

he was lucky to be still alive.' A poet who was a part of de Vere's entourage wrote of this episode in 1606:[93]

> Naked we landed out of Italy
> Enthrall'd by pirates, men of no regard …

Hamlet on his way back to Denmark sent letters to Horatio and the Danish King saying that 'Ere we were two days old at sea, a pirate of very warlike appointment gave us chase …' ending up with Hamlet being 'set naked on your kingdom.' He promised to explain it all later on (Act 4, Scenes 6 & 7). There are various sources for the play *Hamlet,* but none of them contain that stripped-bare-by-pirates episode: it would seem to come solely from de Vere's own life.

An Unacknowledged Child

The good name of de Vere was blasted by his refusal to acknowledge the first child which Anne bore him, which led to stormy gossip about him having been cuckolded. Can one fathom what happened?

There are hints given in *Hamlet*. Hamlet cautions Polonius about his daughter's conception by another, unknown person: 'Have you a daughter? … Let her not walk i' th' sun. Conception is a blessing, but as your daughter may conceive, friend, look to't' (2,2). The distracted Ophelia sings bawdy tales about copulation: 'Young men will do't if they come to't / by cock they are to blame' to which Hamlet responds by comparing her beauty to that of a bawd, sadly concluding 'I did love thee once.' (3,1) Ophelia keeps protesting her innocence, then has a rather unconvincing suicide by falling into a stream beneath a willow tree – compare Anne Cecil dying at the far too-young age of 33.

De Vere departed from England in January, 1575 for a fifteen-month sojourn across Europe. On March 7th the Queen's doctor Dr Master reports that Anne is 'evidently' with child, then on 17th of March de Vere

[93] Poem by Nathaniel Baxter: Anderson, p.113, Whittmore, p.26..

in Paris is happy to be told the news, it makes him a 'glad man.' He sends to his young wife a portrait of himself, the well-known youthful image.

The child was reportedly delivered on 2nd of July, as is noted in Cecil's diary. De Vere was not told the news until September, when he wrote back saying how glad he was to receive such tidings. From this the Ogburns concluded: "Since Lord Oxford had raised no question when he heard, late in September, that the child had been born in July, he had evidently had intercourse with his wife at Hampton Court in October."[94]

Figure: the 25 year old De Vere, painted in Paris (from copy in the National Portrait Gallery)

There is in Cecil's diary a record that Oxford had "confessed to my Lord Howard that he lay not with his wife *but at Hampton Court*" (i.e., *in October*).[95] We gain the impression that the two were not living together. He's left his nineteen-year old wife all alone and what is she supposed to do for all that time?

The next April found de Vere in Paris, where his steward and estate manager arrived from England to visit him. De Vere was advised that

94 The Ogburns, *This Star of England* (online) Chapter 9.
95 Ibid.

the child was not his because it had been delivered in September, not in June. The steward also darkly hinted that Cecil, anxious to have an heir with the great de Vere name, had manipulated his daughter in this manner. After this, de Vere refused to see his wife for the next five years, not even greeting her upon his return to England. He knew, we must presume, that he had not slept with her during the winter-time. When he got back home, all the world wanted to tell him that he was mistaken and that yes she'd been faithful to him. He gave Anne a country house but did not wish to see her.

The testimony of the queen's physician Dr Richard Master is crucial here. He wrote to Burghley on March 7th, telling him that his distraught daughter had requested that he, Dr Master, perform an abortion on her: and that was one week after de Vere had left for Italy i.e. around the 12th -15th of February. What she asked for was some herb or tincture *ad menses promotiones* i.e to restart her periods: "she kept it a secret 4 or 5 days from all persons and that her face was much fallen and thin, with little colour.' She cried in the doctor's presence:

> ... and to say truth, I stand in doubt whether he [de Vere] pass [judgement] upon me and it [the pregnancy] or not. And bemoaning her case would lament that after so long sickness of body she should enter a new grief and sorrow of mind.

Thus in February when her condition of being with child was *first noticed,* she was asking the doctor for something to terminate the pregnancy and restart her periods.

There should have been nothing more gladdening for her than to be with child – who might well become the 18th Earl of Oxford – and should it not have been the best day of her life? Would not all the problems of her difficult marriage be over, if she could make her man happy with this good news? Instead she looks anguished, has kept it a secret for days, expresses doubt to her doctor that her husband will ever believe it is his, and is asking for an abortion!

If the pregnancy was first noticed in February that indicates a midwinter conception, corroborates a September birth and rules out de

Vere's paternity. Soon courtiers were laughing at de Vere, calling him a cuckold. This horrific drama which destroyed de Vere's happiness was an ideal background for the stormy tragedies of the Bard (as in *Othello*).

The Spanish Ambassador Guerau de Spes rightly commented upon Burghley that he was 'a crafty fox, a man of mean sort but very astute, false, lying and full of artifice', that he was a man who played 'tricks' and 'who thereby thinks to cheat everyone, in which to a certain extent he succeeds.'[96] Only years later did de Vere become reconciled to his wife who gave him two more daughters.

A Stormy passion

De Vere became embroiled in a tempestuous affair with a new court beauty, the nineteen-year old Anne Vavasouer, in 1581. She came to star as the 'dark lady' of the Sonnets. He possibly met her when she was much younger in her early teens[97] as indicated in Sonnet 151 where he declares that he finds her irresistible:

'Love is too young to know what conscience is / Then gentle cheater, urge not my amiss / Lest guilty of my faults thy sweet self prove / ... flesh stays no farther reason / but, rising at thy name, doth point out thee / as his triumphant prize. Proud of this pride / he is contented thy poor drudge to be.' He was never sure whether it was love or lust but whatever it was he couldn't resist it: 'The expense of spirit in a waste of shame / Is lust in action.' He just couldn't manage 'To shun the heaven that leads men to this hell' (Sonnet 129).

She delivered their illegitimate child at the royal court! For this the Bard paid a heavy price, first being imprisoned by the wrathful Queen, then exiled from her Court and finally being wounded in the leg by the furious uncle of Vavasouer in a duel. None of that helped his reputation, which already had quite enough scandal swirling round it from his

---

[96] Ogburns, Ibid, p. 249

97 As Andrew Field '*the Lost chronicles of Edward de Vere*' 1990 p.131 has it.

marriage – starring him as the absentee husband alleging he's been cuckolded. As a German source calmly noted:

> The earl of Oxford … is in the Tower for forgetting himself with one of the queen's maids-of-honour, who is in the Tower likewise. This in spite of his having a pretty wife, daughter of the [Lord] Treasurer. But he will not live with her.[98]

After his wife Anne died in 1588 he may have rekindled his love of Anne Vavasouer. She was ten years younger than him and by then was married. His name had been ruined - or so he came to feel - from such double adultery. His anguish was immortalised in the Sonnets 110 / 111:

> Alas 'tis true, I have gone here and there,
> And made myself a motley to the view…
> Thence comes it that my name receives a brand
> Your love and pity doth the impression fill,
> Which vulgar scandal stamp'd upon my brow.

That wasn't the least of reasons as to why he couldn't in the end put his name to the plays. Also, that Sonnet expressed his concern as to whether the most senior noble lord in the country had mingled unduly with the common people. Already he had violated courtly lore by composing plays, not something expected from anyone of noble birth.

Shakespeare was hailed by Ben Jonson as 'soul of the age.' Such an achievement would have necessitated a wide variety of experience, whereby de Vere had 'made myself a motley to their view'.

De Vere died broke, while Robert Cecil died owning three hundred landed estates.[99] The latter had developed quite a skill in relieving English Catholics of their land, homes and property. While de Vere was still a young, trusting Ward of Cecil's, he was relieved of his rightful inheritance, Castle Hedingham, by way of Cecil charging him outrageous expenses for accommodation in the Strand. He had been

98 Newsletter of the Fugger dynasty of international investors: Anderson, p.172.
99 Looney p.214.

born at Castle Hedingham which, when he was aged 11 the Queen came to visit for four days of masques, feasting and entertainment.

When aged twelve Londoners had their first sight of the youthful Earl, as he came into town leading a procession from his ancestral castle Hedingham, while mourning the death of his father in 1562:

> He 'came riding out of Essex' from his father's funeral 'with seven score horses all in black, through London and Chepe and Ludgate, and so to Temple Bar.' (Machyn's Diary 1848, Whittemore, p173)

As an elderly man whose finances were in ruins, having lost his ancestral home, he was wonderfully rescued by Elizabeth Trentham and her most legally competent brother Henry. They managed to sort out the chaos of his properties and legal affairs. Thanks to that wounded leg he could no longer shine as the bright star of the Court, a-dancing, a-jousting and generally travelling around, and instead remained quietly at home through the 1590s.[100] People wondered, what had happened to him? In Hackney 'that Star of England,' quietly retired, was communing with 'the prophetic soul of the wide world / dreaming of things to come' as the experiences of his life became distilled into written-out dramas, his youthful endeavours being finalised into works of peerless perfection. His good friend the Earl of Southampton may have played a part in communicating the play manuscripts to the theatre companies such as The Globe.

The late (posthumous?) *King Lear* play which appeared in 1605 sees the Bard distressed about something: 'Thou art a soul in bliss: myself am bound upon a wheel of fire.' What exactly was the problem? The aged Lear was addressing his youngest daughter Cordelia, after he had handed over land and property rights to the other two of his three daughters. The very idea of owning nothing and being happy is reflected in the folly of King Lear. De Vere's ancestral home of Hedingham had been transferred to Cecil's ownership and thence to de

---

[100] 'Made lame by fortune's dearest spite' - Sonnet 37, and 'Speak of my lameness...' Sonnet 89. In 1585 he wrote to Cecil, "I will attend Your Lordship as well as a lame man may at your house."

Vere's daughters Elizabeth, Bridget and Susan. Perhaps he found this arrangement stressful? Given the way in which de Vere had treated their mother, of refusing to see her for years, and never liking her that much, one might well expect a dearth of filial affection. Or, as some surmise, did de Vere remain alive after his 'death' which the daughters may have found even more stressful?[101] Susan the youngest of his three daughters equates to Cordelia as being the genuinely loving child and who much later on collected together and masterminded the publication of her Father's plays.[102]

The Fool says to King Lear – 'I can tell why a snail has a house.' 'Why?' asks Lear, inviting the reply: 'Why, to put his head in; not to give it away to his daughters'. *Hedin*gham => head-in. After four centuries, we finally get the joke!

Two Italian Texts

If there was a favourite book of de Vere it was the Italian *Cardanus' Comfort,* dedicated to him by its translator Thomas Bedingford in 1573. It discussed how the courtier should behave, that being a kind of ideal Renaissance figure. De Vere's name appeared on the frontespiece, in effect the book's publisher. Its author the Italian Gerolamo Cardano was a mathematician as well as being an expert on how to cheat at games of cards and dice. An early poem by de Vere was inserted into this treatise by its translator.

---

101 As Stefanie Hughes in *Educating Shakespeare, What he knew and how and where he learned it* (2022) argues.

102 Susan de Vere participated in a masque in 1602 performed at court where each masked lady had a 'witty couplet' to recite. (Its author had in the previous summer composed a masque to celebrate Elizabeth de Vere's wedding) Susan was apparently given a cruel epigram which read, 'Nothing's your lot. That's more than can be told / for Nothing is more precious than gold' - alluding to her father having nothing to offer for a wedding-dowry. Compare *King Lear* where the daughter Cordelia tells her father she has 'nothing' to offer him, unlike the other two sisters, and thereby fails to receive any share of his estate. Thus *Lear* must have been composed after 1602. (Anderson 354)

Two Italian Texts

Hamlet's 'To be or not to be?' soliloquy is reckoned to echo the sentiments of Cardanus's Italian book about life, death and how to be a courtier – such that it has often been alluded to as 'Hamlet's Book.' In 1934 a Shakespeare scholar studied the similarities and concluded that, 'without exaggeration, *Cardanus Comfort* is pre-eminently 'Hamlet's book,' since the philosophy of Hamlet agrees to a remarkable degree with that of Cardano."[103] An argument for authorship exists here, as it has long been perceived as having a profound influence upon the composition of the Shakespeare plays and *Hamlet* in particular, as well as the book's English translation being so closely linked to de Vere.

<u>Cardanus</u>

'In holy scripture, death is not accounted other than sleep, and to die is said to sleep ... What should we account of death to be resembled to anything better than sleep?'

For there is nothing that doth more truly prophecy the end of life, than when a man dreams that he doth travel and wander into far countries ...and that he travels in far countries without hope of return.

Only honesty and virtue of mind doth make a man happy, and only a coward and corrupt conscience do cause thine unhappiness.

<u>Hamlet</u>

To die, to sleep ..- no more; and by a sleep to say we end the heartache and the thousand natural shocks that flesh is heir to: 'tis a consummation devoutly to be wished. To die-to sleep – to sleep, perchance to dream; ay, there's the rub; for in that sleep of death what dreams may come..

But that the dread of something after death, the undiscovered country, from whose bourne no traveller returns...'

Thus conscience doth make cowards of us all, and thus the native hue of resolution is sicklied o'er with the pale cast of thought.

Another Italian book translation associated with de Vere was Castiglione's *Il Cortegiano* or *The Book of the Courtier* on 1561 (earlier

103 Hardin Craig, 'Hamlet's Book:' Whittemore p21

quoted, page 31). It refashioned the mediaeval ideal of the chivalrous knight by fusing it with the Renaissance virtues of learning and grace (Whittemore p.19). Its author, a friend and contemporary of Raphael, had been exiled in Spain, where he dramatized the Italian court of Elisabetta - as de Vere did for Elizabeth: their queens Italian and English enjoyed the same name. The book became, in the decade after its translation, 'akin to holy writ for English gentlemen seeking to emulate the sophistication of continental court culture.'[104]

De Vere's extolled this work with the Preface he composed, when merely 22 years of age, finding that its ideals were his: his life-work tried to bring the glory of the Italian Renaissance to England. The *Courtier* appears as one who knew his place in an ordered and heirarchical society. De Vere wrote in his Preface:

> For who has spoken of princes with greater gravity? Who has discoursed of illustrious women with more ample dignity? No one has written of military affairs more eloquently, more aptly about horse-racing, and more clearly and admirably about encounters under arms on the field of battle. I will say nothing of the fitness and excellence with which he has depicted the beauty of chivalry in the noblest persons.

As one of the great works of the High Renaissance it exerted a strong influence upon the courtly ideals of Elizabeth's reign. De Vere's latin translation published in 1571 made it accessible to educated persons throughout Europe. The influence of this text pervades the plays and is reckoned to be, along with the Roman poet Ovid, one of the most seminal texts for his work:

> Without Castiglione we should not have *Hamlet.* The ideal of the courtier, scholar, soldier, developed first in Italy, and perfected in the narrative of *Il Cortegiano,* was Castiglione's gift to the world. Prince Hamlet is the high exemplar of it in our literature. (Drayton Henderson, *Hamlet as a Castiglionean Courtier* (1934): Whittemore, p.20)

---

104 Anderson, p52.

A nobleman who is also a writer must 'take care to keep them [literary works] under cover and let him show them only to a friend who can be trusted,' reckoned Castiglione (Anderson, p.65). It was definitely bad form for a nobleman to publish. De Vere certainly broke that constraint by putting his name to the English translation of *The Courtier* in 1573. His commoner uncle, brother to his mother, was the famous translator, scholar and poet Arthur Golding, who had translated Ovid's *Metamorphosis.* The business of translating books would have come naturally to de Vere from within his own family.

The Unseen Bard

The figure of the Bard has remained unrecognized down through the centuries, and that in a sense is because our notion of *the courtier* has vanished with time. As the royal families of Europe declined in power and gradually also lost any perceived divine mandate, so the courtier ceased to be such an important element in state affairs. That figure had been in part a scholar or leaned sage but was in reality much more than that.

There was a celebrated joisting tournament at which, at twenty-one years of age, one month before he became engaged to Anne Cecil, the young De Vere appeared. One observer noted:

> He controls his foaming steed with a light rein, and armed with a long spear rides to the encounter. Fearlessly he settles himself in the saddle, gracefully bending his body this way and that. Now he circles around; now with spurred heel he rouses his charger. The gallant animal with fiery energy collects himself together, and flying quicker than the wind beats the ground with his hoofs, and again is pulled up short as the reins control him.
>
> Bravo, valiant youth![105]

---

105 Giles Fletcher, Eclogue, Hatfield MSS: a tribute, translated from the Latin, Ward p.61

As one of the participants at the event noted, 'Lord Oxford has performed his challenge at tilt, tournay, and barriers, far above expectation of the world, and not much inferior to the other three challengers', the other three being practiced veterans. 'The Earl of Oxford's livery was crimson velvet, very costly, .. he was the red knight. There is no man of life and agility in every respect in the Court but the earl of Oxford.' (Ward p.60) He became the champion *spear-shaker* of the lists. As a reward, the Queen gave him a tablet of diamonds.

Many years later, after the Spanish Armada's defeat in 1588, in which de Vere had participated, his secretary John Lyly wrote:

> De Vere, whose fame and loyalty hath pierced
> The Tuscan clime, and through the Belgike [Belgian] lands
> By winged fame for valour is rehearsed
> like warlike Mars upon the hatches stands,
> His tusked boar 'gan foam for inward ire
> While Pallas filled his breast with fire

envisaging him as standing on the deck of his ship the *Bonaventura* in the wake of the great English military victory (Whittemore p161).

A decade earlier, Lyly had published his *Euphues the Anatomy of Wit,* often said to be the first English novel. It gave expression to a new literary movement: as Ward tell us of its style, 'It was the wealth of metaphor and rhetoric, the interminable juggling with words and sentences, that appealed so much to the Elizabethans and made Lyly's novel in a single day the most widely read book in the country.' (p.184) He being de Vere's secretary is highly relevant to the Bard's development.

The Queen, fortunately, denied him a military career, no doubt sensing that he was her chief dramatist. As a courtier and a knight, he was one with a flamboyant, theatrical turn of mind. For example, consider the 'Tree of Gold' performance in 1581 to entertain the Queen at the Whitehall Tiltyard. The crowd of spectators silently watched de Vere emerge from a magnificent tent as the 'Knight of the Tree of the Sunne.' He sat down under the tree while his page boy approached the

Queen and made a speech, concerning how the knight would defend this mythic tree. Elizabeth personified the tree's majesty, and Oxford was the champion willing to live or die in her defence. The symbolic phoenix came into the story, a bird reborn though fire. Then de Vere mounted his horse and rode to defend his title:

> By the tilt stood a stately Tent of Orange tawny Taffeta, curiously embroidered with silver and pendants on the Pinnacles very slightly to behold. From forth this Tent came the noble Earl of Oxenford in rich gilt Armor, and sat down under a great high Bay-tree, the whole stock, branches and leaves whereof were all gilded over, that nothing but Gold could be discerned.

By the Tree stood twelve tilting-staves, all of which likewise were gilded clean over. 'After a solemn sound of most sweet music, he mounted on his horse... After the speech to the Queen with great honour he ran, and valiantly broke all the twelve staves.' The pageant ended with an unseemly crush, as crowds rushed in to tear up the tree and tent, each trying to grab some gold. The Poet was using solar-gold symbolism here to delight Her Majesty.

The End

Why does everyone say *Hamlet* is Shakespeare's best play? It is a terrible meditation upon Death – the two kings are killed, as are the two brothers Laertes and Hamlet, the two ambassadors Rosenkrantz and Guildenstern are murdered, the two women close to Hamlet, Gertrude and Ophelia, are also killed, the wise old counsellor Polonius dead: they all somehow bring death to each other. And through this there emerges onto the stage of history the *first unhappy intellectual,* Hamlet the Dane. We're left with the strange impression that Hamlet is a real character, more real than the ordinary people we meet or more real than other characters in the plays. At last we're fathoming why this is – at least from one point of view it is the Author himself, who has verily stepped into his last play.

De Vere afficionados take quite personally the dying words of Hamlet as applying to them, as he urges Horatio 'to tell my story.' They do not wish to accept the awful finality of 'The rest is silence', No! Four centuries later, Oxfordians endeavour to rescue from oblivion the name of this supreme genius, this pre-eminent Englishman.

De Vere died on the 24th of June 1604 under mysterious circumstances – no will, no funeral, no tombstone – then a few months later 'sometime during the latter half of 1604 an ornate print of *Hamlet* appeared' which strangely synchonized with the galactic supernova 'Kepler's Star.' It lit up in the heavens from October of 1604 - which Hamlet would no doubt have appreciated. Many were the prophecies composed, based upon this brightly burning new star as it lit up in-between Jupiter and Saturn, after those two had just made a triple conjunction, i.e. they had met together three times in the heavens. The Bard did not allude to this spectacular sight, despite having kept up remarkably with other scientific advances of the day, strongly suggesting that he was indeed dead. No more of the 'newly-corrected' plays were published and 'no new Shakespeare plays would appear in print between 1604 and the months leading up to the 1623 First Folio.'[106]

We are dazzled by the brilliance of his life.

1623 / 2023

The present quattrocentenary of the monster hoax, *the greatest literary cover-up of all time,* is *the* moment in history to discard the mountainous backlog of books claiming the Stratford fellow as author. '*The Man who was Never Shakespear*e' by Pointon 2011 has finally clarified the identity of this Stratford-upon-Avon businessman who came to practice in a modest and limited manner as an actor in London. This character may be of interest by virtue of the way he doubled as a Stratford businessman with a family, sometime butcher, grain salesman and moneylender -

106 Anderson, p.360.

then appeared in the mid-1590s linked to the 'The Lord Chamberlain's Men' troupe of actors. After four centuries, that identity is now sufficiently in focus that the possibility of him ever being literate can be eliminated. This means that everything at Stratford-upon-Avon, the entire Shakespeare tourist industry, is fake! Let us hope that this 400-year anniversary will open up for literary minds the whole larger question of authorship, 'the unseen immensity of the question of his identity.'[107] A good place to start could be by dating the plays, hitherto constrained by assumptions about a Stratford authorship.

On the 400th anniversary of the publication of the great work in 2023, let us finally encourage unconstrained debate over who are the main candidates. Their contributions are far from being mutually exclusive: Christopher Marlowe, Edward de Vere, William Stanley and Mary Herbert.[108]

It was the golden age for plays and literature, in which the very language of England underwent a phoenix-like rebirth. The poet Thomas Heywood in his *Apology for Actors* (1607) looked back at the Elizabethan era and described how it had transformed and refined what had been a rough, uncouth language:

> Our English tongue, which hath been the most harsh, uneven and broken language in the world ... is now by this secondary means of playing, continually refined, every writer striving in himself to add a new flourish unto it: so that in the process .. it is grown to a most perfect and composed language, that many excellent works and elaborate Poems writ in the same, that many nations grew enamoured of our tongue.

Let us give credit where it is due. To remind ourselves of what is at stake, here are the concluding words of Thomas Looney's 1920 opus which first identified de Vere as being *the Man*:

107 politicworm.com/2020/10/17/why-is-it-taking-so-long/

108 The play *Upstart Crow* (London, 2022) reviewed four main candidates: the Stratford fellow, then de Vere, William Stanley and Lady Herbert.

> Speaking no longer from behind a mask or from under a pseudonym, but in his own honoured name, Edward de Vere, Seventeenth Earl of Oxford, will ever call mankind to the worship of truth, reality, the infinite wonder of human nature and the eternal greatness of man.

Hallelujah! The Bard explained the purpose of his works, as being *medicinal*:

> I must have liberty
> Withal, as large a charter as the wind
> To blow on whom I please, for so fools have…
> Invest me in my motley, give me leave
> To speak my mind, and I will through and through
> Cleanse the foul body of th'infected world
> If they will patiently receive my medicine

As you like it 2,7

The Book of Proverbs tells us, 'As a man thinketh with his heart, so is he.' The characters in these plays somehow speak from their inmost being, from their hearts, and there is something about them that cannot ever fade away.

'Shake-speare' wove many plots, but the greatest plot he ever made concerned his own identity. That remains today as England's greatest mystery. In the contemporary words of Derek Jacobi, patron of the De Vere Society:

'We all love Shakespeare – whoever he is.'

Sonnets quoted:

81, 107 - page 34
125 - page 41
33, 73 - page 50
53 - page 51
14, 55 - page 52
97, 100 - page 53
77 - page 54
1, 4 - page 58
5,80 - page 59
135 - page 61
151, 129 - page 78
10, 111 - page 79
37, 89 - page 80.

Biblio

Anderson, Mark *Shakespeare by Another Name* 2005.

Asquith, Clare *Shadowplay The Hidden Beliefs and Coded politics of Shakespeare* 2005

Evans, A.J., *Shakespeare's Magic Circle* 1956

Looney, J. Thomas, *"Shakespeare" Identified* Centenary Edition 1920, 2018.

Malim, Richard *The Earl of Oxford and the Making of Shakespeare* 2011

Michell, John *Who was Shakespeare?* 1996

The Oxfordian, Vol. 21, 2019.

Pointon, A.J. *The Man Who was Never Shakespeare* 2011

Rollett, John *William Stanley as Shakespeare, Evidenc of Authorship*, 2014

Roper, David *How Science proved Edward de Vere was Shakespeare* 2018

Titherley, *Shakespeare's Identity*, 1952

Ward, Captain B.M., *The 17th Earl of Oxford* 1928

Whittemore, Hank *100 Reasons Shake-speare was the Earl of Oxford* 2016

Williams, Robin, *Sweet Swan of Avon Did a Woman write Shakespeare?* 2006

politicworm.com by Stefanie Hughes and hankwhittemore.com/, the latter giving '100 reasons why Shakespeare was the Earl of Oxford.' hankwhittemore.com/2011/12/08/ hankwhittemore.com/tag/first-folio/ susandevere.wordpress.com/ susandevere.wordpress.com/ facebook.com/TheMarySidneySociety?ref=hl

****

Early Tributes to the Bard

1. 1578 Address by the poet-scholar Gabriel Harvey, during a visit by de Vere, the Queen and top officials to his home in Cambridge, praising the 28-year old Edward de Vere:

"Thy splendid fame, great Earl, demands, even more than in the case of others, the services of a poet possessing lofty eloquence. Thy merit doth not creep along the ground, nor can it be confined within the limits of a song: it reaches in wonder as far as the heavenly orbs [...] England shall discover in you her homegrown Achilles [...] Pallas will be at hand to instruct your heart and mind.

O great-hearted one, strong in thy mind and thy fiery will, thou wilt conquer thyself, thou wild conquer others; thy glory will spread out in all directions beyond the Arctic Ocean; end England will put thee to the test and prove thee to be a native-born Achilles. Do thou but go forward boldly and without hesitation: Mars will obey thee, Hermes will be thy messenger, Pallas striking her shield with her spear shaft will attend thee, thine own breast and courageous heart will instruct thee.

For a long time past Phoebus Apollo has cultivated thy mind in the arts! English poetical measures have been sung by thee long enough! Let that courtly epistle – more polished even than the writings of *Castiglione* himself – witness how greatly thou dost excel in letters. I have seen many Latin verses of thine, yea even more English verses are extant; thou hast drunk deep draughts not only of the Muses of France and Italy, but has learned the manners of many men, and the arts of foreign countries...[109]

It was a summons to Martial action, but also viewed de Vere as a literary genius, assuming that he had written many poems in Latin and English.

2. 1586 William Webbe *A discourse on English Poetry*, 'I may not omit the deserved commendations of many honourable and noble lords and Gentlemen in her Majesty's court, which, in the rare devices of poetry, have been and yet are most skilful; among whom the Right Honourable Earl of

109 Translated from the Latin: Whittemore, p.64; Malim, *The Earl of Oxford & Making of Shakespeare*, p.77-8.

Oxford may challenge to himself the title of the most excellent amongst the rest.'[110]

3. 1586 A Mr Angel Day dedicated his bestseller *The English Secretary* (concerning how to write letters) to de Vere with the comment; 'the learned view and insight of your Lordship, whose infancy from the beginning was ever sacred to the Muses.' (Whittemore, p.95)

4. 1589 Lord Lumley *The Arte of English Poesie* - another fine tribute to Edward de Vere's literary standing, with a hint of the secrecy involved:

> And in her Majesties time that now is are sprong up another crew of Courtly makers, Noble men and Gentlemen of her Majesties owne servantes, who have written excellently well as it would appeare if their doings could be found out and made publicke with the rest, of which number is first that noble Gentleman Edward Earle of Oxford.

5. 1590 Edmund Spencer's *Faerie Queen* had a dedicatory sonnet to the Earl of Oxford, describing a mutual love between de Vere and the Muses:

> ... th' antique glory of thine ancestry
> Under a shady veil is therein writ,
> And eke [moreover] thine own long living memory
> Succeeding them [de Vere's ancestors] in true nobility:
> And also for the love, which thou dost bear
> To th' Heliconian nymphs - and they to thee -
> They unto thee, and thou to them most dear...

Something is being written 'under a shady veil' whereby memory of his ancient, noble, ancestral lineage works through him: whereby there is a mutual relation of De Vere with the Muses of Parnassus!

Spencer's *Teares of the Muses,* dedicated to Alice the wife of William Stanley. alludes to rivalry between Spencer and de Vere, 'those two brilliant court poets' (Ward, p.339)

---

110 'A sufficient number of his poems is extant to corroborate Webbe's comment, that he was the best of the courtier poet of the early days of Queen Elizabeth' - *Dictionary of National Biography*; Looney 2019, p.228.

6. 1595 William Covell's *Polimanteia* managed to imply in a semi-cryptic manner that the poet Shakespeare was 'our de Vere' – ie the poet Edward de Vere, the Earl of Oxford.

7. 1598, Francis Meres' *Palladis Tamia* was registered for publication. It placed Oxford at the top of a list of brilliant playwrights as 'the best for comedy among us' and has the first mention of 'Shakespeare' as a playwright, attributing twelve plays to him.

8. 1610, John Davies *To our English Terence, Mr Will Shake-speare* indicated that the Bard was close to royalty: "Some say good Will (which I, in sport, do sing) / Had'st thou not plaid some Kingly parts in sport / Thou hadst bin a companion for a King" John Michell reckoned that would apply better to Stanley, whose name was 'Will' and who had a top royal lineage. (possibly also relevant: 'Terence' in Roman times was a slave who allowed it to be thought that he was the author of works composed by aristocrats).

9. 1612 Henry Peacham's *Minerva Britannica* concerned Emblem-designs. Its frontespiece depicted a 'hidden hand' writing: 'mente.videbori' The letter 's' would have to be added to make 'mente vidboris' meaning 'in the mind thou shalt be seen,' which doesn't convey too much. But it forms an anagram by taking out the letters 'De Vere' leaves 'Nom tibi' i.e. 'your name'. Peacham greatly admired Oxford as a poet so the meaning here is plain, with 'your name is De Vere' alluding to something hidden behind a curtain. A Latin sentence twining around the encircling laurel wreath says 'His genius abides.'

10. 1613 A play by George Chapman, *The Revenge of Bussy D'Ambois* contained the first eulogy in print to Oxford (This was the year after Robert Cecil's death):

> I overtook, coming from Italy,
> In Germany, a great and famous Earl
> Of England; the most goodly fashioned man
> I ever saw: from head to foot in form

Rare and most absolute; he had a face
Like one of the most ancient honoured Romans
From whence his noblest family was derived;
He was besides of spirit passing great
Valiant and learned, and liberal as the sun,
Spoke and writ sweetly, or of learned subjects,
Or of the discipline of public weals:
And 'twas the Earl of Oxford. (2.4.84-95)

It describes an encounter in 1576, when the young playwright encountered the 26-year old de Vere on his journey returning back to England from the Continent. [111]

11. 1622 Peacham's *The Compleat English Gentleman*

Reviewing what he reckoned had been *the golden age of British wit and poetry*, Peacham perceived de Vere as the major star, whom he listed first:

> ...truly a golden Age (for such a world of refined wits and excellent spirits it produced, whose like are hardly to be hope for, in any succeeding age) above others, who honoured poesie with their pennes and practice (to omit her Majesty, who has a singular gift therein) were Edward Earle of Oxford, the Lord Buckhurst, Henry Lord Paget: our phoenix, the noble Sir Philip Sidney, M. Edward Dyer, M. Edmund Spencer, Master Samuel Daniel, with sundry others. (p.95)

There was no mention of 'Shakespeare,' and likewise he omitted that name from the second and third editions of his book (1624 and 1634) - even after it was cited in the great Folio of 1623!

12. 1624 Thomas Vicars' *Manual of Rhetoric* listed Britain's top poets making no mention of Shakespeare – a year after the First Folio! - but then four years later a new edition stated, very deliberately,

> to these [names] I believe should be added that famous poet who takes his name from 'shaking' and 'speare.'

111 Mark Anderson, *Shakespeare by another Name* 2005, P.109; Whittemore Ibid., p276.

It could hardly be made it any clearer, that Vicars did not believe a poet by the name of Shakespeare had existed, and was somewhat indicating that he knew who was behind the pseudonym.

Love/death chronology

1554 Queen Elizabeth imprisoned in the Tower

1575 Child of Anne Cecil de Vere is born

1576 De Vere returns to England

1581 De Vere imprisoned in the Tower, after Anne Vavasour has his child

1588 Anne Cecil dies

1591 De Vere marries Elizabeth Trentham

1592 Raleigh imprisoned in the Tower

1593 Marlow killed

1597 Ben Johnson imprisoned for a seditious play

1598 William Cecil lord Burghley dies

1598 Ben Johnson imprisoned for killing a fellow actor

1601 Essex executed

1603 queen Elizabeth dies

1604 de Vere dies

1612 Robert Cecil earl of Salisbury dies

1618 Walter Raleigh executed

1620 Mary Pembroke dies

New Words & phrases

Its hard even to think without using Shakespearean phrases: *What's done is done * of a sudden * Wild goose-chase * Money's worth * With bated breath * A sorry sight * Heart's content * Well behaved * Love letter * Cold blooded * Eaten out of house and home * Household words* As Bernard Levin once memorably expressed the matter:

> 'If you cannot understand my argument, and declare ``It's Greek to me'', you are quoting Shakespeare; if you claim to be more sinned against than sinning, you are quoting Shakespeare; if you recall your

salad days, you are quoting Shakespeare; if you act more in sorrow than in anger; if your wish is father to the thought; if your lost property has vanished into thin air, you are quoting Shakespeare; if you have ever refused to budge an inch or suffered from green-eyed jealousy, if you have played fast and loose, if you have been tongue-tied, a tower of strength, hoodwinked or in a pickle, if you have knitted your brows, made a virtue of necessity, insisted on fair play, slept not one wink, stood on ceremony, danced attendance (on your lord and master), laughed yourself into stitches, had short shrift, cold comfort or too much of a good thing, if you have seen better days or lived in a fool's paradise -why, be that as it may, the more fool you , for it is a foregone conclusion that you are (as good luck would have it) quoting Shakespeare; if you think it is early days and clear out bag and baggage, if you think it is high time and that that is the long and short of it, if you believe that the game is up and that truth will out even if it involves your own flesh and blood, if you lie low till the crack of doom because you suspect foul play, if you have your teeth set on edge (at one fell swoop) without rhyme or reason, then - to give the devil his due - if the truth were known (for surely you have a tongue in your head) you are quoting Shakespeare; even if you bid me good riddance and send me packing, if you wish I was dead as a door-nail, if you think I am an eyesore, a laughing stock, the devil incarnate, a stony-hearted villain, bloody-minded or a blinking idiot, then - by Jove! O Lord! Tut tut! For goodness' sake! What the dickens! But me no buts! - it is all one to me, for you are quoting Shakespeare.'

1582 Hekatompathia – 100 sonnets The passionate century of love. De Vere married Elizabeth Trentham – she sets him up in Hackney where he can write. After he dies, she sells her Hackney Place. She gets royal permission to sell 'king's Place' so she can buy back castle Hedingham – profits from Sonnets to do this. May 1609 – sonnets entered into Stationer's Register using Mr W.H. frontman (William Hall, recently married in Hackney, hence 'all happiness' June 1609 sells Hackney to Fulke Greville then buys back castle Hedingham. Lord Burghley forced him to sign over the Hedingham home in trust to his daughters. Sonnets written in king's Place, Brooke house, Hackney near Kenninghall Road and lea bridge roundabout. Sonnet 37: de Vere made lame. British Museum has inventory of goods in Hackney House, the countess of Oxford. Wriothesley (pronounced 'Rosely')

Part 2

THE GUNPOWDER PLOT

- England's *Original* State Fabricated Terror Event

- Plots have I laid, inductions dangerous

  - Richard III, Scene 1

-

- Who is so gross / That cannot see this palpable device? / Yet who's so bold but says he sees it not?

  - Richard III Act 3 Scene 6

-

Tudor Plots

The inconsistencies, not to say absurdities, of a plot based on a mine which we can safely say never existed, and on a quantity of gunpowder which would never have exploded ....' – Francis Edwards[112]

The Tudor state had a problem in legitimising itself, after it had banned and criminalised what had been the religion of England for a

---

112 Edwards, *The Enigma of the Gunpowder Plot: the 3rd Solution* (2008), p.214. In 1969 he had published *Guy Fawkes, the Real Story of the Gunpowder Plot,* thus much of his life was occupied with the topic.

thousand years. It had been decreed that the reigning monarch was the head of the Church and citizens were allowed no options in this respect. Whereas France in contrast, a Catholic country, had the Edict of Nantes which allowed citizens to practice a Protestant religion. No other European nation was as oppressive and intolerant of religious diversity as England.

William Cecil had been a trained lawyer with long experience of the secret workings of government. 'For fifty-two years William Cecil and his son Robert effectively governed England. In the process, they created a dynasty so powerful that members of the Cecil family have remined a periodic force in British politics ever since.... Under the Cecils a spy service grew up that became an invaluable tool of intimidation and suppression throughout Elizabeth's reign.'[113] The poet Edmund Spencer, author of the celebrated *The Faerie Queene*, in praise of Elizabeth, had this satirical comment upon William:

> So did he good to none, to many ill
> So did he all the kingdom rob and pill
> Yet none durst speak, ne none durst of him 'plain,
> So great he was in grace and rich through gain

after which, he was obliged to emigrate to Ireland.[114]

The Tudor dynasty ended in 1603 with Queen Elizabeth having produced no heir and the crown passed onto James Stuart, formerly the king of Scotland. Arguments as to why he should inherit the crown were less than conclusive and did he perhaps need a 'founding narrative' that would cause people to rally round him? Because that is indeed what happened.

Government-generated plots could be most convenient - as a French writer commented:

---

113 Clare Asquith *Shadowplay, The hidden Beliefs and coded Politics of William Shakespeare,* 2005, p.12

114 Spencer, *Mother Hubberd's Tale* 1591; Edwards *op.cit.,* p.306.

> ...plots undertaken under Elizabeth and James I had this feature in common, that they proved, one and all, extremely opportune for those against whom they were directed.[115]

while in relation to the Gunpowder Plot, the author Gerard found -

> The wide prevalence of the belief, that previous plots had owed their origin to the policy of the statesmen who finally detected them.[116]

He quoted Lord Castlemaine that 'making and fomenting plots was then in fashion.' Soon after the Gunpowder Plot was dramatically 'discovered' a letter from London to a correspondent abroad stated:

> Those that have practical experience of the way in which things are done, hold it as certain that there has been foul play and that some of the Council secretly spun the web to entangle these poor gentlemen, as did secretary Walsingham in other cases.[117]

The king's cunning and Machiavellian intelligencer, Robert Cecil the Earl of Salisbury, appeared to many as having been:

> a person deeply read in politics; who had inherited the double spirit of his predecessor Walsingham, knew all his tricks and legerdemain, and could as seasonably discover plots as construe them.[118]

Could the Gunpowder plot have been another one of this kind? There was to start with a lack of perceptible motive:

> ...The absence of any possibility that the cause could be benefitted which the conspirators had at heart. (Gerard, p.38)

Catholics were oppressed, quite intolerably so. House searches were routine, holding Mass was a crime, having a crucifix on one's mantelpiece could spell jail while being found with a rosary was even worse. Catholics were confined to within five miles of their homes: 'England is one vast prison for all who profess the faith,' lamented one

---

115 M. l'Abbé Destombes, '*La persécution en Angleterre sous la règne d'Elizabeth*', 1863, p.176; quoted in John Gerard, *What was the Gunpowder Plot? The Traditional Story tested by original Evidence* 1897, p.14.

116 Gerard, Ibid., p.14.

117 Letter of 10th December 1605, quoted in Gerard p.43.

118 *A Plain and Rational Account of the Catholic Faith,* (Anon) Rouen 1871, p.197; quoted in Gerard, Ibid., p.50.

Catholic priest.[119] But, however one views the situation, blowing up Parliament would only have made things worse - far, far worse. Even were the King to be killed, there was no possible Catholic successor.

It is hard to say what proportion of English people then remained as Catholic, but suffice to say that any option of restoring a Catholic monarch was long gone. The most that English Catholics could have hoped for was an edict of toleration, and the new king – himself Catholic by birth - might possibly have been able to manage that, had it not been for the Gunpowder Plot.

England was no longer at war with Catholic Europe and there was no obvious terrorist threat. And yet, in March of 1605 Cecil assured the Venetian ambassador that 'a good Catholic must nurture in himself the firm resolve to be ready, for the preservation of his faith, to attack the life and government of his natural sovereign.' One must concur with Clare Asquith that: '… the statement implies that Cecil was aware of the conspiracy from its very beginning, at least nine months before the projected explosion.'[120]

After Cecil's passing in 1613, the verdict of John Chamberlain, a perceptive commentator, was:

> He juggled with religion, with the king, queene, theyr children, with nobilitie, parlement, with friends, foes and generally with all.[121]

What an epitaph!

The Plotters: Double-Crossed?

If a group of thirteen desperate men were working together, risking their lives and those around them, to devise a plot involving one-and-a-half tons of gunpowder, they would have had to have had some aim, some desired outcome. Mere rage and despair can drive one person to

119 Asquith, *Op. cit.*, p.155.
120 Asquith, p.325.
121 Edwards 2008 op cit., p.3.

act, but cannot hold a group together in a condition of total secrecy – there would have to be some hope of a possible outcome which they shared, to act thus. Six of the plotters had earlier been complicit in the failed Essex Revolt: which would leave them prone to being manipulated by having the threat of a treason accusation brought against them. The ringleader of the new plot Robert Catesby was probably in prison when James came to throne, as one of the malcontents rounded up to prevent possible trouble. He had to sell his lovely estate at Chastleton in Oxfordshire to pay the fine for that complicity.[122]

Three days after the November 5th event (or rather non-event, because nothing happened), the main suspects (aka 'plotters') Catesby and Thomas Percy were shot and killed by government troops in a last stand at Holbeach near Stratford. The two emerged from the house, unarmed except for their swords, and offered no resistance, standing back-to-back with Catesby holding a crucifix – a Catholic symbol. One would have expected the local sheriff in charge of this operation to want them alive, for which he would have gained credit from London. Surrounded by a hundred or so government troops, the unarmed couple could easily have been arrested *had this been desired.* Killing them meant that no-one would know what had been their intention, no-one would get to hear their version of events.

That is a *normal feature* of modern state-fabricated terror events because it enables the government's narrative to be spun.

The heads of Catesby and Percy were cut off and impaled upon the railings of Parliament House. The soldier who had shot them both at Holbeach House received a considerable pension of two shillings a day for life as a reward, which is about twice what a skilled labourer would earn. Sceptics wondered as to why this was? On the accepted story these men would have been better taken alive.

The Yorkshireman Thomas Percy seems to have played the role of a double agent, being espied coming and going from Cecil's house:

---

122 M.R. Beardsley, *The Gunpowder Plot Deceit* 2018 p.117.

> Sir Francis Moore .. having some occasion of business with him at midnight .. and going thus homeward from York House to the Middle temple at two, several times met Mr Percy coming out of that great statesman's [Robert Cecil's] house, and wondered what his business should be there.[123]

What indeed?

<u>Figure</u>: the plotters

Percy, a Protestant who had converted to Catholicism, had earlier been chosen to visit James while he was the King of Scotland, before 1603. Percy carried a secret correspondence to the King from the Earl of Northumberland and made three such visits. He was well-received by the king, who gave him solemn promises about how well the Catholics would be treated once he was King of England. Yes they would be protected! He took Percy by the hand and 'swore to carry out all he had promised.' Coming back to England, Percy spread the good news. Later on, the King would never admit to having given these promises.[124] Thus there was quite an intense interaction going on between these two men, Percy and the King, they *knew each other* well.

---

123 Geoffrey Goodman op. cit. I, p.104-5.
124 Frazer, p.50.

Some months before the event, the Earl of Northumberland had Percy appointed to the Honourable Corps of Gentlemen at Arms, which would have enabled him to rent the little room in Westminster. Then on 25th October Percy was issued with an official pass declaring that he was travelling on 'the King's especial service' such that 'all mayors, sherrifs and postmasters' would 'provide him with three good horses all along the road.' He could travel freely and be provided with horses![125] That shows a high level of trust *from the King*. We are here reminded of King James' sly reply, when he was asked, how come there were so many Catholics in his court? He replied that he was 'using tame ducks to catch wild ones.'

It would seem that the King and Percy got on together over several years. The account of Percy being seen coming and going from Cecil's mansion in the Strand around midnight just before the event may perhaps begin to make some sense. To whom was he loyal? It was imperative that he be shot dead at Holbeche right away after the event, before he had a chance to speak about what had, or had not, happened. Both him and Catesby had to be shot because they knew too much.

A deathbed confession by Robert Catesby's servant George Bartlett revealed that on *three* occasions Catesby had been brought into Salisbury House, always privately via a back door.[126] Cecil had also managed to get his hooks into Catesby it would appear. That would presumably account for why Catesby advised the band that they should go ahead with the 'Plot' even after (as we'll see) they knew it had been discovered.

A lot of pressure had been put on the plotters to incriminate Catholic priests by their 'confessions' but they would not. A letter from Cecil complained of this obstinate refusal by the conspirators: 'yea, what torture soever they be put to.'[127] At their trial the conspirators pleaded,

---

125 Beardsley Ibid., p.123.
126 'At least towards the close of the play Cecil made direct contact with Cartesby': Edwards Op. cit., pp.42, 44, 116.
127 Antonia Frazer *The Gunpowder Plot* 1996, p.243

'not guilty.'[128] On Jan. 27, 1606, eight of the survivors, including Fawkes, were convicted and sentenced to be hanged, drawn and quartered.

The Jesuit priest Father Garnet was ensnared by Catesby 'confessing' to him about the plot and so lost his life: bound by the strict rules of the confessional, he could not inform the state about whatever he had been told, and that was deemed to be treasonous. He wrote, while imprisoned in the Tower of London, 'Master Catesby did me much wrong ... He did it to draw in the others.'[129] Catesby had married a Protestant and their son Robert was baptised at their Protestant parish church just a few years before the plot, leaving room for doubt over his alleged fervent Catholicism.

There are several accounts of 'plotters' who seem to have been in touch with Cecil. Thus one of them, Francis Tresham is said to have had privileged access to Cecil's house 'even at midnight' and that he and a companion were 'the secretary's instruments.'[130] He is said to have died conveniently after November 5th but reports exist of his being allowed to escape to the Continent, maybe as a reward for his assistance (Beardsley, p120).

The whole drama went straight into the Book of Common Prayer and stayed there for three centuries: how evil Catholics had wickedly schemed to blow up the House of Lords but fortunately by Divine Providence the King (the new Stuart ruler, James I from Scotland) had divined the plot and thwarted it. For Catholics all across England the event spelt ruin, the extinction of their hopes.

---

128 Frazer Ibid., p.265.
129 Martyn Beardsley, Ibid, p.118.
130 A claim made in *The Politician's Catechism* of 1662: Beardsley, p.119.

Three Viewpoints

'According to the orthodox, old-fashioned view Salisbury discovered the conspiracy, a second judgement is that he nourished it, and a third that he invented it.' — Archbishop Matthew[131]

There have been three generally-held perspectives on the Gunpowder Plot:[132]

1. That it was what it appeared to be, a plot devised by fed-up Catholics to blow up the houses of Parliament. It was not a success.[133]
2. Ditto, but the whole thing was followed by the Crown's intelligence having its own agenda: so the plot was allowed to run its course – almost.
3. The plot was instigated by Robert Cecil, King James' chief intel officer and so the plotters were essentially dupes, recruited and used. It was a total success.

9/11 conspiracy-theorists may note that the last two resemble LIHOP and MIHOP positions: 'Let it Happen on Purpose' versus 'Make it Happen on Purpose,' depending on how active a part is played by the national intelligence agency. The second of these positions has been well summed-up by Clare Asquith:

> The plot was infiltrated and controlled by Robert Cecil from its earliest stages, and its carefully stage-managed discovery delivered the decisive *coup de grace* to the English Catholic cause ...[It was] the last in a long line of assassination plots that historians can now demonstrate were deftly infiltrated, nurtured and exposed by the intelligence service. But in spite of attempts at the time, and ever since, to blame the whole thing on Cecil, the evidence is inescapable:

131 Letter in the Sunday Telegraph, 2.11.69, quoted in Francis Edwards, ibid.

132 The historians S.R. Gardiner ('*What the Gunpowder Plot was* 1897) and Father John Gerard (*What was the gunpowder plot?* 1897) argued in the 19th century as to whether there really had been a plot: the latter as a 'no-plotter' reckoned it had been a government fabrication.

133 For an endorsement of the official, government narrative see Gardiner, Ibid.

> the plotters were utterly dedicated men; most of them died resolutely defending their actions.[134]

Concerning the plotters, she helpfully added:

> The plotters were not hardened soldiers of fortune but a cross-section of Catholic gentry from the Midlands, their respectability marred only by the presence of the shady Thomas Percy, the most likely to have fallen under government influence.. among the plotters was Sir Everard Digby, young, handsome, happily married to an enchanting wife, 'the goodliest man in the whole court.' All had suffered loss of estates or prospects for the sake of their religion…

<u>Figure:</u> Guy Fawkes is inspired by the Pope and the Devil, but Divine Providence espies the Plot just in time. Inside the entrance are the barrels of gunpowder covered by sticks.

---

134 Asquith, *Shakespeare and the Resistance*, 2005, p.104.

We're not in a hurry to agree with Lady Antonia over Thomas Percy being a 'shady' character - he had negotiated in good faith with the king of Scotland James VI for an England at peace with itself with religious toleration. The Stuarts were after all traditionally Catholic. And he remained in good standing with James when he became King of England.

What is more or less the second view has been well expressed in the comprehensive work by Lady Antonia Fraser, '*The Gunpowder Plot, Terror and Faith in 1605*' (1996), highly acclaimed by reviewers, where she advocated the view that 'foreknowledge is not fabrication.' We will start off in a moment by accepting her thesis, and see how well it works.

The French generally speaking inclined to the 3rd option, viz that the British Crown had brewed up the plot by manipulating a group of fiery malcontents. As a 19th – century French source reckoned: 'The greedy and haughty minister Cecil seems to have been the Soul of the plot, and to have discovered it himself at the right moment, after having presented to the weak mind of James 1, the danger to which he was being exposed from the Catholics.'[135]

The third view has been well argued in modern times by Webster Tarpley, the US political commentator and 9/11 theorist, in talks and radio interviews.[136] The definitive opus could be that by Francis Edwards[137] entitled *The Third Solution.*

Lady Antonia Frazer divided theorists on this topic into 'pro-plot' and 'no-plot' groups. That is not very helpful as no-one disputes that a plot existed: the question is, who brewed it up?

---

135 'Le mininstre cupide et orgueilleux, Cécil, semble d'avoir été l'Ame du complot,et l'avoir découverte lui meme au moment propice, après avoir présenté a l'esprit faible de Jacques 1. Les dangers auxquels il était en but de la part des Catholiques.' –M.Bouillet, *Dictionnaire d'Histoire et de Géographie*.1851.

136 For Tarpley interview on 'cloak and dagger' radio station, see Appendix (transcript at progressivepress.com/ peaceweek/cloakandgunpowder.html

137 Francis Edwards op. cit., 2008.

The Story as Told by Lady Antonia Frazer

The prime initiator of the plot appears as being Robert Catesby and he it was who inspired others to join. The charismatic Earl of Essex who had been urging religious toleration for England was executed in 1601. Catesby, inspired by this promise of toleration for his co-religionists, joined what came to appear as a revolt or rebellion, though Essex had not intended it that way. He induced some other Catholics to join amongst whom were Thomas Percy, Thomas Winter, John Wright, and Lord Monteagle, most of whom are said to have later joined the Gunpowder Plot. Catesby managed to escape with a ruinous fine.

Is it here credible, that being thus greatly under suspicion for disloyalty and lucky to escape with their lives, they would want to assemble in secret for an even worse plot, the only likely outcome of which would be to lose their heads and be remembered with everlasting horror?

The 2nd Earl of Essex. Robert Devereaux, advocated an easy-going religious tolerance between Catholics and Protestants. Many of the 'plotters' had rallied to his cause.

Plotting supposedly began on May 20th 1604, when Catesby, Tom Wintour, Jack Wright, Thomas Percy and Guido Fawkes met at the Duck and Drake pub in London. Somehow the charisma and force of Catesby's personality carried them along: Wintour agreed that 'I told him yes, in this or what else soever, if he resolved upon it, I would venture my life.' They hoped for some foreign help, which never arrived. Catesby had a house in Lambeth where the gunpowder would be stored. A Mr Ambrose Rookwood was asked to obtain the gunpowder, allegedly for use by some English troops abroad.

Rather casually, Lady Antonia Frazer admits that this huge amount of gunpowder was dud i.e. it could never have gone bang: the powder was described officially as 'decayed:' 'This powder ... would not have exploded anyway,' because she reckoned 'the powder had once again separated into its elements' and 'Guido had simply not realised the fact.' (p.226) Gunpowder takes about two years to 'decay'. If its three simple components – potassium nitrate, sulphur and carbon – are mixed and well ground together in the correct proportions then the powder should stay 'live' unless it is allowed to become damp. As we will see, what the plotters may have acquired consisted of what was called 'corn-powder', this being a non-explosive version of gunpowder with bigger grains.

This is the weakest part of her narrative: that this vast convulsion in national affairs, this horrible trauma which had such huge repercussions, was based upon dud explosive?

In December of 1604 the plotters allegedly started to dig an underground passage from a room which Thomas Percy had managed to rent, adjacent to the House of Lords. They had to abandon the project several months later. That was originally quite major part of the narrative, but Frazer here concedes that:

> This mine [i.e., tunnel] was most likely a mythical invention, used by the government to spice up the official account of the narrowly averted danger. For one thing, no traces of this famous mine were ever found. (p.133)

She here alludes to the demolition of the old House of Lords buildings in 1823, when it was ascertained that no trace of the tunnel could be found. The alleged tunnel began from a room which had been part of a little house adjacent to the House of Lords, this being rented by Thomas Percy since May of 1604. He had business in the House and via his patronage by the Duke of Northumberland was credibly able to do this. However it was a single-bed room and nowhere near large enough to store barrels of gunpowder in, let alone for seven plotters to stay in it while they dug through a wall. Generally speaking one can't just start digging a hole in a wall of rented accommodation and hope not to be detected! The room could be let out to tenants when Parliament was not assembled but otherwise it functioned as a robing or withdrawing-room for the Lords.

Guy Fawkes

'A man of great piety, of exemplary temperance, of mild and cheerful demeanour, an enemy of broils and disputes, a faithful friend, and remarkable for his punctual attendance upon religious observances.' – such was the testimony of Father Greenaway concerning Guido or Guy Fawkes.[138] Another testimony concerns how he avoided disputes, and was 'pleasant of approach and cheerful of manner, opposed to quarrels and strife … he was a man liked by everyone and loyal to his friends.' (Father Tesimond)[139]

He was brought up as a gentleman of good family from Yorkshire whose father Edward Fawkes held the office of Registrar and Advocate of the Court of the Cathedral Church. He was educated in a free-school near the city of York. Both of his parents were Protestant so his early education was within the Protestant faith. But his Father died when he was only eight years old and his mother remarried to a Catholic, so his further education would have been Roman Catholic.

He enlisted as a soldier of fortune in the Spanish army at Flanders. He became well-known to English Catholics and after the death of Queen Elizabeth he was despatched by Sir William Stanley and Owen from Flanders, to join an embassy to Philip II of Spain. To quote further from Father Greenaway, his society was 'sought by all the most distinguished in the archduke's camp for nobility and virtue.' Terms of a peace treaty with Spain were being negotiated and the question was, whether toleration for Catholics would be included? A truce was signed in July of 1604. By then Guy Fawkes was back in England, and next thing we

138 David Jardine, *A Narrative of the Gunpowder Plot*, 1857, p.38.
139 Beardsley p.11.

hear is, he's looking after a lodging rented by Thomas Percy adjoining the palace of Westminster. And what exactly did he think he was doing there? That, alas, is a question with no answer.

The Tunnel

On 24 May, 1604 the plotters hire as a lodging Mr Whynniard's tenement,[140] rented by Thomas Percy, which lay close to the House of Parliament:

> when .. they had entered into traitorous considerations and were guilty of treason, that Percy, who hired the house adjoining the parliament, did put them upon this particular plot.
>
> – Geoffrey Goodman the Anglican Bishop of Gloucester.[141]

It seems odd that a group of Catholics were allowed to rent a room adjacent to the Houses of Parliament; but they were here assisted by Sir Dudley Carleton, one of Cecil's top diplomats. Carleton was rewarded for this by subsequent promotion to Foreign Secretary as Viscount Carleton. Such promotion of key operators is a central feature of state-fabricated terror.

The tunnel was allegedly dug from that rented room, excavating it for two and a half months, January to March 1605 and disposing of all the earth and rocks in a nearby garden. That was a visible and frequented patch of land in-between the River Thames and Parliament. None of the plotters had any experience in such digging. The tunnel story enhanced the perceived 'wickedness' of the plotters, as working away *underground* in the *darkness*: the conspirators were regularly termed the 'Miners' in parliamentary debate. Guy Fawkes started to narrate the tunnel story during his fifth interrogation, when stretched out upon the rack – that being *the* most feared of torture implements. All seven miners 'lay in

---

140 The room was managed by Mr Whynniard, who had the title 'keeper of the wardrobe.'
141 Godfrey Goodman, *The Court of King James the First,* 1839, 2011, p.105; quoted in Gerard, 1896.

Percy's house' or so he then averred. Someone had added to his written confession in handwriting other than Fawkes own that it was a mine leading 'to the cellar under the Upper House of Parliament.'

The alleged digging of the tunnel served a vital purpose. It *involved* the plotters, who otherwise might merely have appeared as a bunch of angry dreamers from around the Midlands of England, who had not spent much time around Westminster and who had just talked of doing a deed which they probably believed would never happen. To quote the perceptive Mr Beardsley, 'working on the mine ties them physically to the attempt to blow Parliament up, puts them physically on the spot and demonstrates clear intent.'[142]

Figure: The 'Cellar' under the house of Lords (source: Gerard)

The tunnel dig came to an end as a thick wall was encountered in the way – which of course no-one would have expected. Directly above them, they then realised, was a cellar, or rather a huge storage-chamber, underneath the main House of Lords chamber and could they not use that instead? It was a large ground-floor room 77 feet long and 24 feet wide having four main doors to give access. Originally it had been the palace kitchen but was then being used for storing coal. Guy Fawkes was sent round to check it out and he finds it is available. Percy rents

142 Beardsley Ibid p.110.

this also! If it was so easy for Mr Fawkes to just potter round and 'discover' this room, how come the plotters had not noticed it before? It sounds just like the place to hide away thirty-six barrels of gunpowder for half a year[143] - no-one would ever notice! Guy Fawkes had allegedly been given a key to this large room by Thomas Percy, but this is very unlikely: there were too many doors, and it was a public access place where coal was bought and sold.

No part of this tunnel story makes any sense.

If the authorities had made up the entire tunnel story – as they had – then people were going to start wondering, what else had they lied about? If the plot was what they said it was, why would they need to torture Guy Fawkes to get him to confess about a tunnel for which no material evidence existed?

A group would meet in the summer of 1605 in London – Catesby, Thomas Wintour and others, by way of getting their swords engraved, with 'the story of the passion of Christ' richly engraved upon the hilt. Was this by way of preparation for the Gunpowder Plot? That hardly seems credible. Rather, they were preparing to go out to fight in Flanders on the Spanish-Catholic side. Without going into details it was legitimate for English Catholics to do this.[144]

The Monteagle letter

On 26th of October, an unsigned letter was delivered to Lord Monteagle at his residence in Hackney, obscurely revealing some terrible plot that would harm the next Parliament. It was apparently delivered by some stranger, who was not recognized by the servant to whom it was handed. Who could it be? The letter started,

---

143 Official reports have the powder brought in 'about Easter' and covered with firewood to conceal them.

144 Edwards, *Real Story of Gunpowder Plot*, 1969, p.126

The Monteagle letter

> My Lord, out of the love I bear to some of your friends, I have a care of your preservation. Therefore I would advise you, as you tender your life, to devise some excuse to shift of your attendance at this Parliament...they shall receive a terrible blow this Parliament, and yet they shall not see who hurts them.

He took this mystery letter to Cecil in Whitehall, who - evidently not in a rush - showed it a few days later to the King. It was presented as being enigmatic such that only King James was clever enough to figure out that it involved an attack upon parliament. And yet, contrary to what might have been expected, *no* measures were then taken for the security of the House, and the conspirators - who had got to hear of Monteagle's letter – allegedly breathed again.

The narrative has no one at first understanding the meaning of the opaque letter until it was shown to James, who "did upon the instant interpret and apprehend some dark phrases therein, and thereupon ordered a search to be made". 'Thereupon' is hardly the appropriate word here, because days went by before anything was done.

In fact, *ten days* went by after that letter had been received before anything was done - viz., the search through the rooms and cellar on the afternoon of November 4th. Cecil explained this delay by saying that it afforded more time for the plot to 'ripen.'[145] His use of this expression indicates that he knew there was a plot - and presumably, that he was in charge of its timing. We concur with Lady Antonia Frazer that, 'Salisbury with the Monteagle letter between his fingers now felt confident of commanding the situation.'

As Lady Antonia Frazer rightly explained,

> Monteagle – and Salisbury – were of course bound to produce an author, or at least a suspected author, of the letter which they themselves had concocted. (p202)

---

145 Frazer p.181. Cecil told the Privy Council that he delayed the search in order that "such as had such practice in hand might not be scared before they had let the matter run on to a full ripeness for discovery." Gerard, p. 133.

The Monteagle letter

> The Monteagle letter was fake and not only Monteagle and Salisbury knew it was fake. It was brought into being for a special purpose. Nothing else makes any sense of Salisbury's extraordinary urbanity – one might even call it complacency – in the days following. There was certainly no sense of impending danger in his conduct, such as might have been expected if the letter had presented him with a genuine mystery. (p187)

Monteagle was handsomely rewarded for producing the letter, being given lands worth £200 a year and an income of £500, plus he was extolled by Ben Jonson as 'saviour of my country, thee alone.' This must have been music to his ears, given that only a mere few years ago he had been imprisoned for his part in the Essex Rising. No wonder people suspected him.

Who could have let Monteagle into the secret of the Powder treason? The Plotters included his closest friends and relatives. There were indications that 'Monteagle probably knew far more in the months leading up to the Powder treason – long before the mysterious letter appeared – than he would afterwards ever admit.' (p186) This was one of the more suspicious features of the official story.

Figure: The theme of 'divine providence' shown as the Monteagle letter is delivered to King James.

Monteagle's servant evidently had a link to the plotters via these close relatives and was thereby able to advise them of this betrayal. The Government knew! So why did that not lead to the cancellation of their plans? Catesby told his group decided that the letter had been rather vague in its warning, and so it was OK to press on. That was the last chance for the plotters to save themselves - had they desired to do so.

Lord Monteagle was a Catholic, so one might have expected a degree of enmity from Robert Cecil. James I had referred to him as 'odious' and yet Cecil clearly protected him in the ensuing storms. As well as giving him a fine pension, Cecil ensured that his name was removed from documents relating to the Gunpowder Plot. He appears as having been a middle man, giving 'helpful' guidance to the plotters as regards how to proceed, while keeping Cecil informed. On the night before the trial of the plotters took place, Cecil sent a letter to the prosecuting council instructing them to ignore any such growing suspicions:

> You must deliver in commendation of my Lord Monteagle words to show how sincerely he dealt....because it is so lewdly given out he was once of this Plot of Powder and afterwards betrayed all to me.[146]

The letter was written in a hand unknown and had no address, date or signature. It was received by Baron Monteagle while dining in a house in Hackney, which was then just outside of London. He only visited it very rarely and had not been there for over a month. How did the unknown messenger know where he would be? The messenger had to be someone who knew well the habits of the Baron, in which case how could he not have been recognized by the servant who accepted the note? If the letter was so important, why was it not delivered personally? Francis Tresham was widely suspected as the author of the letter, he being a good friend of Monteagle – but if so why would he not just have given the warning orally, which would have avoided the betrayal of the Plot of which he was then accused? Nothing made sense.

Let's backtrack a little. Monteagle married a daughter of Sir Thomas Tresham, and thereby became connected with several Catholic families,

---

146 Cecil to Coke, d. Jardine, *Criminal Trials,* 1832; Gerard p. 146.

especially those of Thomas Winter and Robert Catesby. His correspondence in this period shows that he was especially close to these people: Catesby, Tresham and Winter. The latter, Thomas Winter, had employed him as a secretary and personal assistant - while he was trying to invite the king of Spain to invade England with an army, promising support from Catholics. So, yes this was treason, colluding with the Queen's enemy! Monteagle was as guilty of plotting as anyone could be, and had enjoyed a spell in the Tower for his part in the Essex revolt, back in 1601. He was thereby an ideal 'tame duck' to use James' phrase to catch and incriminate other Catholics.[147]

Figure: the blue plaque at Hackney – with a wrong date!

On Saturday 26th of October he did two things both having no apparent reason or motive: firstly, he directed that a supper be prepared at Hoxton (modern Hackney in North London) where he had not been for more than a month. Secondly, at 7 pm he sent a servant on an 'errand' go out and he conveniently met the unnamed stranger, which sounds as if they had an appointment to meet – at 7 O'clock. The servant just happened to 'bump into' the unnamed stranger, who gave him the all-important, unsigned letter. Monteagle promptly handed the letter over to Thomas Ward, one of those he was having dinner with, telling him to read it out for

147 David Jardine, *A Narrative of the Gunpowder Plot*, 1857, pp.78-92.

everyone at the table to hear: Ward being a close friend of the alleged conspirators and could be relied upon to tell them what had happened, which he is said to have done the next day.[148] Everything here sounds like a pre-arranged theatre.

Cecil himself remarked that the letter was 'in a hand disguised.'[149] Modern handwriting analysis has confirmed this, but has also indicated that it was written by Cecil himself! Miss Joan Cambridge, a professional document examiner accustomed to giving expert evidence in courts of law, was the chairman of Scientific Graphologists and one of Britain's leading authorities on handwriting. She was allowed by the Public Records Office to scrutinise the Monteagle letter, and she compared that with handwriting in letters by Robert Cecil, Francis Tresham and Father Garnett. The latter two had been traditionally fingered as suspects for the letter.

Her final conclusions were:

* The Monteagle letter was 'beyond doubt' written by someone attempting to conceal their hand;

* Those who had by tradition been suspected as authors - Francis Tresham or the Jesuit Father Garnett - could not have written it;

* Cecil could 'beyond doubt' have written it;

* As to whether Cecil actually wrote it, she replied: 'Probably he did. It is a 70 per cent probability. I can't go further than that because there are special factors of the ink and paper having aged. But I'm reasonably satisfied in my own mind that he did.'[150]

These are pointing to Cecil as mastermind of the Plot.

---

148 Beardsley, p.52.
149 Letter from Cecil to Sir Charles Cornwallis of 9 November: Beardsley, p.55.
150 askwhy.co.uk/analogiesandconjectures/gunpowderplot0.php#Graphology . Ms Cambridge's analysis was also described in *The Gunpowder plot, Narrative of Oswald Tesimond alias Greenway,* 1973, Appendix 2.

Gunpowder

Who actually saw the powder, the great stack of barrels, anyway? What proof is there from anyone outside Cecil's circle or sphere of influence?[151]

Dudley Carleton, the Earl of Northumberland's secretary, wrote to John Chamberlain a week after the event:

> The fire which was said to have burnt our king and council hath been so hot in these two days past in every man's mouth, is but ignis fatuus or a flash or some foolish fellow's brains to abuse the world. For it is now confidently reported that there was no such matter, nor anything near it more than a barrel of powder found near the court.[152]

Such Catholic scepticism was rife in the aftermath of the event – somewhat as today, when Muslim nations tend not to believe the official 9/11 story.

In theory the government held a monopoly on gunpowder but it seems to have been fairly easy to acquire. It was part of the equipment of every soldier and there were powder mills at various sites around London. But the amount here involved was impossibly large – estimated as one month's supply for the entire British army! No-one is reported as seeing any of the heavy barrels as they were carried clunking up the steps from the river to the Parliament building – carried by a shady group of Catholics, known for their part in the Essex plot!

The so-called cellar was a large, basement or a ground floor room to which many people had access, yet the barrels were allegedly stored there for six months. It was an open room which had been the kitchen and was now used for general storage, eg for a pile of coal. It is doubtful whether the several doors had locks, or that there was a 'key' for entrance. Were there indeed twenty barrels first brought in and then more added in July to make a total of thirty-six? Can anyone believe that they were stored there for months without being noticed? Also, the

151 Beardsley, Ibid, p.113.
152 Francis Edwards, *Guy Fawkes the Real Story of the Gunpowder Plot,* 1969, p.138.

obtaining of such large quantities and its transport from Lambeth on the southern side of the River Thames up to the Houses of Parliament greatly strains our credulity. How could they have concealed carrying all these barrels into the large, ground-floor room without a single eyewitness report in that crowded area of town? None of that makes any sense.

Parliament opened on the afternoon of November 5th with the King due to speak. He was addressing the new parliament, so the whole place would have been packed out with security guards, especially in view of the dire warning message that had been received. Were all those barrels of live gunpowder still in place directly underneath the House of Lords? Surely, not! No-one ever saw heavy barrels being moved into place, just as no-one saw them being removed. Nor was any panic recorded that afternoon when everybody assembled into the Great Hall on the first floor, as there assuredly would have been had they been told that barrels of explosive were directly beneath them. This is what is nowadays called a psy-op.

As John Gerard noted, concerning the various testimonies about the gunpowder, 'No witness speaks as if he had himself set eyes upon it, but we are always referred to someone else.' (p.86) He sagely added, 'From the moment of the 'discovery' the discovered gunpowder disappears from history.' (p.141)

Over the centuries various people have tried in vain to check the government records for this elusive gunpowder. The investigator Hugh Williamson was startled to find -

> As has already been noted, the Ordnance accounts of the stores for this period are missing. But concerning the gunpowder, no question appears ever to have been asked, whence it came or who furnished it .. no mention is discernible of the augmentation of the royal stores by so notable a contribution as this would have furnished.'[153]

---

153 H.R.Williamson, *The Gunpowder Plot,* 1957, p.251,3, 7.

He noted how one person connected with the Tower of London had applied for a warrant to 'investigate the disappearance of gunpowder from the Royal stores.' That didn't get very far:

> The fact is, no one, apparently, apart from the trusted officials immediately involved, ever saw the barrels or knew if there was, indeed, gunpowder inside ... not only are the gunpowder records now missing, but the government of the day showed a remarkable unwillingness to allow William Brouncker to inspect the records going beyond 1604.

Later on a report appeared in the *Daily Telegraph* for 1978 which described finding the original Office of Ordinance receipt, dated 7th of November 1605, for 1,800 lbs of 'decaied corn-powder.'[154] That is less than a ton and a mere fraction of what had been alleged. This announcement surely has to represent a turning-point in the entire debate, indicating that the whole thing was in some way theatre, a mere semblance of a plot, which successfully created horror simply because it was so well done. Cornpowder has the ingredients of gunpowder, but not ground together well enough to be explosive. The Office of Ordnance record, of powder being as it were returned to the Government, is almost the only objectively known fact about the Plot.

When one throws in this fact that the gunpowder used was dud, it was 'cornpowder' ie low-grade stuff that would burn and could not possibly have exploded – then the alleged plot becomes somewhat absurd. Was there really a group of furious dissidents, galloping up and down England, sworn to secrecy, renting rooms as close as possible to Parliament, trying to dig a huge tunnel to get underneath Parliament – and all the time their gunpowder was dud? Would life and limb have been risked without anyone checking that it 'worked'?

---

154 Daily Telegraph May 4 1978: official records from The Office of ordinance dated November 7th, 1605, found that it was 1800 lbs of 'cornpowder,' that had 'decaied.' See Appendix for the text. Money had been paid (15s 6d) 'to move the gunpowder to the Tower,' indicating that 'his Majesties store' for gunpowder was in the Tower of London.

If those barrels had actually existed – if we suppose this – then an order early on November 5th would have been given that no-one was allowed to enter the House of Lords building until the barrels had all been removed: they would have been carefully removed and placed upon the grass or garden outside, near to the riverside. While being guarded by the army, astounded Members of Parliament would have viewed them plus any members of the public who had gathered on that day. Then they would have been transported a few at a time to the Office of Ordinance. None of that happened, of course, because it was just an illusion.

Figure: What Never Happened on November 5th, an imaginary drama

Here is an image of the discovery of the plot. All your life you had believed that something like this had taken place! It depicts what Britons have been told happened - over the last four centuries – whereas no-one is on record, as having witnessed such a scene. Shocked members of parliament peer out of windows, while to the left members of the public watch in amazement as the barrels of gunpowder are removed from the cellar and carried away. At bottom right Guy Fawkes is being arrested, his plan having been foiled.[155]

Is the narrative credible? Here's a catholic view:

> "We may here pause to review the extraordinary story to which we have been listening. A group of men, known for as dangerous characters as any in England, men, in Cecil's own words, "spent in their fortunes," "hunger-starved for innovations," "turbulent spirits," and "fit for all alterations," take a house within the precincts of a royal palace, and close to the Upper House of Parliament, dig a mine, hammer away for over two months at the wall, acquire and bring in four tons of gunpowder, storing it in a large and conspicuous chamber immediately beneath that of the Peers, and covering it with an amount of fuel sufficient for a royal establishment—and meanwhile those responsible for the government of the country have not even the faintest suspicion of any possible danger. "Never," it is said, "was treason more secret, or ruin more apparently inevitable," while the Secretary of State himself declared that such ruin was averted only by the direct interposition of Heaven, in a manner nothing short of miraculous."

John Gerard, What was the Gunpowder Plot? p.71

The Midnight Hour

For anyone telling this story the main problem lies in the radical absence of direct evidence. The government tells its version of events and various persons are tortured until they come out with an account

155 Here is John Gerard's remorseless logic: 'Neither can it escape observation that whereas the powder was discovered only on the morning of November 5th, the peers met as usual in their chamber that very day. It cannot be supposed either that four tons of powder could have been so soon removed, or that the most valuable persons in the State would have been suffered to expose themselves to the risk of assembling in so perilous a situation. However this may be, from the moment of the "discovery" the discovered gunpowder disappears from history.' (*What was the Gunpowder Plot?* P.137)

that agrees with it, while the few people who may have known of what was planned to happen are quickly shot.

There *did not exist* in the Parliament building an underground cellar away from prying eyes where thirty-six barrels could have been hidden away. This may remind us of modern state-fabricated terror events where the *mysterium* has to remain hidden, the conjuring-trick cannot be revealed. After the alleged discovery of the plot, the cellar and the area around it were cordoned off so that nobody outside the government was allowed in.

The primal image of this event is of Guy Fawkes at midnight on November 4th / 5th in a cellar underneath Parliament near to the barrels of gunpowder, or sometimes he is outside by a door about to enter. He was apprehended by a group of night-watchmen led by Sir Thomas Knevett inspecting the premises - with no sign that they required a key or anyone's assistance when inspecting the large, ground-floor room. One might have hoped for testimony from one or two of those men as regards what they saw? Did they judge that gunpowder was present? Their testimony concerning that amazing moment would be unforgettable! But of course they remain silent. They are mere stage-props in a theatre, who then fade away.

Few today will believe that the night-watch investigating the vaults of Parliament around midnight just happened to come across Guy Fawkes making his final checkup: catching him red-handed 'emerging from the vault', carrying a lantern, matches and some gunpowder in his pocket. (The last of these sounds remarkably like the planted 'clues' which appear in modern state-fabricated terror events, e.g., British Islamic terrorists are normally apprehended with some bottles of hydrogen peroxide 'found' in their home.)

That group of night-watchmen were the only real witnesses to what happened. The Plot was an event which did not happen with powder that could not have blown up, so - what could they have seen? We'd prefer to have statements signed by several of them, testifying that they observed so many barrels containing some powder, at such and such a place and time, together with testimony of why they believed - if they did - that it was gunpowder. Instead all we have is a seemingly pre-arranged narrative extracted under torture, after the main witnesses such as Percy and Catesby had been killed off.

On another version, Guido Fawkes was arrested in his room, i.e., that rented by Thomas Percy. Asked about the fuse to ignite the explosion, Mr Fawkes stated that 'he threw the torchwood and match out of the wyndowe in his chamber, neere the parliament house towards the water side;' from which Edwards inferred that he was captured in his chamber and not in the cellar (p.204). When first apprehended 'his initial attitude suggested one who had nothing to hide …he showed all the fearlessness of a good conscience' (p.282). We will never hear what Fawkes himself reckoned was going on. That is always the case with state-fabricated terror: one never gets to hear the viewpoint of the 'patsy.' The pictures of Guy Fawkes being captured *never* show him inside that ground-floor cellar.

Figure: Knevett and his men capture Guy Fawkes; with his key, lantern, boots and spurs. The midnight hour is indicated by the stars in top right-hand corner.

One would have liked to hear the opinion of Mr Whynniard, who apparently rented out both the little house and the cellar vault to the plotters. When on November 4th the King's Chamberlain was inspecting the vault, he – according to the official narrative in the *King's Book* – saw the huge pile of faggots and asked Mr Whynniard what they were for?[156]

156 See eg Beardsley pp. 60, 120.

Why, the cellar was rented out by Percy came the reply. Mr Guy Fawkes was then espied lurking in the corner. With Mr Whynniard in so central a position, so well able to assess whatever was happening, we are hardly surprised to hear that he dies immediately after November 5th. He died of shock, poor fellow.

Mrs Whynniard sounds like a fairly sensible and un-tortured witness. Following her husband's untimely demise, she informed her inquisitors that Guy Fawkes had kept his rent payments for the room right up-to-date, and further that he had had workmen in there doing repair work to the house on that very last day, November 4th! We may here quote Mr Beardsley again: 'for Fawkes to bother with repairs to a house he was about to blow up – and to invite outsiders into the plotter's lair at this late stage – is almost beyond belief.'[157]

The King's Story

State-fabricated terror will enhance funding for the security forces, out of gratitude for their protection and to make sure it doesn't happen again, even though it is they who have actually perpetrated the event. Thus the Gunpowder Plot 'immensely increased Cecil's influence and power, and, for a time, even his popularity.' (Gerard) He was awarded the prestigious Order of the Garter at Windsor Palace. Likewise Sir Thomas Knevett, in charge of security for the Parliament building - who somehow failed to hear about a group of shady characters burrowing away in a tunnel and then moving dozens of barrels of explosive right into the cellars underneath Parliament over several months – was promoted to being Baron Knevett and made a Member of Parliament. The perpetrators of state-fabricated terror are rewarded and promoted, to keep them quiet.

The official narrative supposedly composed by King James was known as the 'King's Book'. Called *The Gunpowder-Treason, with a discourse on the manner of its discovery,* it gave to the King credit for

157 Beardlsey, p.90.

discovery of the Plot:

> How the king was Divinely illuminated by Almighty God, the only ruler of Princes, like an angel of God, to direct and point as it were to the very place, to cause a search to be made there, out of those dark words of the Letter [the Monteagle letter] concerning the terrible blow…'

There was a moment when decisive action was required of the King, when after midnight on November 5th he was rudely awakened by a crowd bursting into his bedroom. Sir Thomas Knevett, Justice of the Peace for the District of Westminster, had arrested Guy Fawkes, then returned back to 'the King's Palace' where he and his men met the Lord Chamberlain and Cecil. They duly woke up the King to tell him what has happened, by which time it was 4 am.[158] These top-level diplomats, Cecil, the Lord chamberlain and Sir Thomas Knevett 'immediately warning the rest of the Council that lay in the house, as soon as they could get themselves ready, came with their fellow counsellors to the King's Bed-chamber' and told him of their shocking discovery.

What then does the King do? Had the story really happened, a major sequence of decisions would have been required of him: soldiers to protect the barrels of live gunpowder, steps to cancel that day's sitting of parliament, somebody to verify if there really was live gunpowder in the barrels, and then for soldiers at dawn to begin removing the gunpowder from the building. *None of these things happened*. We're not even told that the King expressed surprise. The text instead glides straight from that bedroom scene into the interrogations of Guy Fawkes during the day - whereby he seemed remarkably casual and not-guilty in his replies - then it proceeds up to Warwickshire and the events at Holbeche. Did the account written by King James entirely omit his decisive contribution, in the form of any orders he gave or judgements he made on the morning of the great day?[159] Or, could it be that it was all pre-arranged?

---

158 *History of the gunpowder Plot written by King James* extracted … by Montague, bishop of Winchester, 1867, p.228.

159 For the King's narrative see e.g. Beardsley, op.cit., Appendix.

Let's backtrack a bit. What, on the story, caused sir Thomas Knevett to venture into 'the cellar' and discover thirty-six barrels of gunpowder, on the crucial day November 5th when Parliament was due to re-assemble? For the narrative to make sense - or as much sense as it ever would - the discovery of the gunpowder has to synchronise, more or less, with the arrest of Guy Fawkes and that in turn has to synchronise, more or less, with the re-assembly of Parliament. Ten days earlier the warning was delivered by hand to Lord Monteagle ('... they shall receive a terrible blow this Parliament and yet they shall not see who hurts them'), after which a leisurely five days go by until November 1st when the King is shown the missive and sagely decrypts it. Then another leisurely four days go by, before the King appoints someone - and that is the Lord Chamberlain (Thomas Howard, the Earl of Suffolk), to inspect the huge room directly beneath the Parliament chamber. On the afternoon of November 4th he sagely espies a pile of 'billets, faggots and coals' in a corner, as well as a tall, suspicious-looking fellow hanging around.[160] He reports this back to King James, who decides that a more thorough search is warranted, however someone else would have to do it. Enter Sir Thomas Knevett with his assistants, who are instructed to search the pile of faggots in the cellar from top to bottom. By this time it's midnight. Before entering the building, Knevett and his men espy the man whom Suffolk had spotted earlier (see above illustration). And how did they recognise him? Why, they did so because he *looked suspicious*. The proverbial image of Guy Fawkes here appears, wearing boots, spurs and cloak and holding a lantern. That had to be him! Sure enough, upon arresting him they found he had a box of matches!

One would expect a search for any treasonous equipment to be carried out in the daytime, not the middle of the night. But, the story of the discovery of the gunpowder had to join up as closely as possible with catching Guy Fawkes red-handed. The two had to be one event. There is no point asking the question, What was he doing lurking about the Parliament at midnight, inside or even outside it, standing by a door? After all, nothing would be ignited until the afternoon of November 5th. The two narratives had to synchronise, however implausibly: discovery

160 But, that was the *King's Book* story, whereas in a letter send abroad to various ambassadors, Guy Fawkes was not then seen. (Beardsley p.56)

of the powder plus catching *the Villain,* and for maximal impact they both had to happen on the day that Parliament was due to re-assemble.

This is drama, this is *theatre,* and it has been *designed.*

A Modern View

In 2005, Webster Tarpley gave an epic 400-year anniversary presentation of the topic on the US 'cloak and dagger' radio station[161] and my account here has been based upon it. A year earlier, Tarpley noted, Cecil had been busy weaving one of his anti-Catholic plots:

> The month before that in April, one of Cecil's spies by the name of Henry Wright reported to him that he had a subagent by the name of Davies who was working a Catholic treason plot, a sting operation to incriminate priests. He should be able to incriminate up to 60 priests he reckoned. The reply came back that not that many would be needed but they had top-level Jesuits and seminary priests. Davies replies that he needs a pardon in writing before he will do anything, and he gets it, dated 25th April, 1604.[162] Thus Cecil is running the plot a year and a half before the thing comes to the surface.

As regards the event itself:

> It looks also like this guy Catesby is a double agent, and we've got Sir Dudley Carlton who has helped them who is one of Cecil's main diplomats, who helps them rent the first basement that they try to tunnel from. Now there are other people, we can't go into all of them, but you've got this group of ex-cons in effect, in the witness protection program, you've got double agents, you've also got a couple of fanatics. You've probably got Guy Fawkes as a fanatic, a dupe, a patsy in that sense.

161 Given to our 9/11 Truth group in London. See Appendix for a radio talk he gave on the 400th anniversary..

162 Gerard pp.94-5; report to Sir Thomas Challoner for Cecil, PRO Calendar of State Papers Domestic, James 1, Vol 8, p.99

> Now a couple of weeks before November 5th when the Parliament is supposed to meet, this Catholic nobleman Lord Mounteagle comes forward and he says to Cecil, "I just got a letter that says I shouldn't go to the opening of Parliament because it might be dangerous," and he shows him the letter. This is called the famous Mounteagle Letter. So Cecil waits four or five days until he can meet the King. Cecil shows it to the King, and says, "Your Majesty, I got this strange letter from Lord Mounteagle, what could it mean, that we shouldn't go to the opening of Parliament? I really can't figure this out."
>
> And James said, "My God, they're going to blow up the Parliament." Now it turns out that James I, when he was in Scotland he was very unpopular, there were numerous attempts to kill him. And one of the attempts to kill him was allegedly a gunpowder plot. They tried to blow up James and his father, so he's used to this ...

King James' father Henry Stuart (lord Darnley) was blown up by gunpowder when James was merely 8 months old. To quote a recent account, while Henry Stuart was convalescing, 'What he didn't know was that while he had been recovering his enemies had been filling the cellars of the house with gunpowder.'[163] A prequel to the Gunpowder Plot story! His castle exploded at 2 am ., with a sound that reverberated throughout Edinburgh. That was in 1567. Thus his son James 1st of England could be very susceptible to the notion, that someone was prepared to do that to him. His family-trauma memory was reactivated, causing him to believe the 'Gunpowder Plot.'

Propaganda about the event was used to unify the people against Catholics, with state-sponsored holidays in which effigies of Guy Fawkes were burned on public bonfires, to celebrate the foiling of the evil scheme. Up until the 1950s it was illegal *not* to celebrate the November 5th holiday each year, and there was a special church service on that date – alluded to by King James as 'Cecil's Holiday.'

---

163 Tudorsociety.com 'Murder of henry Stuart.

Two Fabricated Narratives

The insightful Jesuit Father John Gerard published in 1896 his *What was the Gunpowder plot?* to which the Oxford professor of history Samuel Gardiner replied a year later with his refutation, *What the Gunpowder plot was.* Then Gerard replied with *The Gunpowder Plot and the Gunpowder Plotters*. These two Gerard books are the most insightful works on the subject. It takes courage as well as insight to penetrate official British mendacity and one is grateful for what he achieved.

Thus, Martyn Beardsley in his recent opus states, 'I felt that Gerard's case deserved to be brought before a modern audience.'[164]

There were two main 'confessions' out from which, Gerard explained, the official narrative had been spun: the *Declaration of Guy Fawkes* and the *Confessions of Thomas Winter*. These were, he argued, inauthentic. The first draft of Guy Fawkes *Declaration* appeared on 8th of November, unsigned, then a signed version appeared on the 17th.

That earlier version had included Guy Fawkes' account of how he had stood close to the King at a wedding party.[165] It was the Earl of Montgomery's wedding, held earlier that year. One can appreciate why that was omitted: the last thing the authorities wanted was people talking about how the number one 'Villain' and the King had been standing next to each other at a wedding, that same year! It is an iron rule in modern state-fabricated terror that the 'terrorist' is *known to the authorities* beforehand.

Thus, Robert Catesby accompanied James on a hunting trip, a mere week or so before the event.[166] We would have appreciated a bit more detail here. One senses an untold story, where alas to quote *Hamlet*, 'the rest is silence.' It seems that at least two of the main plotters were well-known to the king.

---

164 Beardsley, op. cit. p.viii.

165 Nicholls, *Investigating the Gunpowder Plot,* 1991, p.26.

166 Beardsley, Ibid., p.55.

As an example of the tampering involved with the documents, Gerard cited the case of Hugh Owen, an exile then living in Flanders who was 'a kind of agent general on the Continent for English Catholics.' (Gerard, p.11) Cecil had written to the judge-interrogator Coke: 'You must remember to lay Owen as foul in this as you may'[167] – and the final version of the Confession did well and truly tar Owen with Gunpowder-plot guilt: "Winter is made to declare, in the most ample manner that Owen was thoroughly committed to the worst part of the treason, that Faukes was sent to the Low countries to acquaint him with the conspirators proceedings, and did so; and that Owen "seemed well pleased with the business." (Gerard, 1897, p.18). Have these people no shame?

The original Guy Fawkes testimony made no mention of Hugh Owen, but in the later more expanded version on the 17th his name duly appeared.

Several specimens of Thomas Winter's handwriting remain today in the Public Record Office, on the basis of which Gerard was able to conclude that Winter/Wyntour had *not* written the confession attributed to him. He had been injured on November 8th at the Holbeche House incident by a bullet through the right shoulder, after which he could not write for some time. When on November 25th he signed a document it was evidently done 'with pain and labour.'

His judge and interrogator Edward Coke averred that he had written out his Confession on ten pages in a neatly flowing hand – with a note appended,

> Delivered by Thomas Wynter, all written in his own hand, 25th November, 1605 – Edward Coke

But the writing was, as Gerard remarked, in a hand resembling that of Winter *before he was wounded*; also it was composed by a more fluent and practiced writer.[168]

---

167 Gerard 1896, p.12

168 Gerard's conclusion that the Thomas Wynter confession was faked or at least extensively doctored was endorsed by Hugh Williamson (*The Gunpowder Plot*, 1951 p.195) based on handwriting analysis.

He always spelt his own name 'Wintour' as likewise did his two brothers, so could he have forgot the spelling of his own name when making his official confession? As to why he thus misspelt his own name, we concur with Mr Beardsley's sage judgement that 'Thomas Wintour has sent a message down the centuries, telling us that he was coerced into his confession and we shouldn't believe a word of it!'[169]

His confession appeared just as the official *King's Book* was being finalised. Its original was dated 25th of November, whereas the final version for the press (of which a copy exists in the Public Record Office) was oddly dated 23rd. An original has to be earlier in time than a copy. This latter version was not in Winter's handwriting. The 'original' version was signed. Concerning the mendacity here involved, Gerard states:

> We have undeniable proof that the statesmen of the period had the means at their command, of investing fiction with an air of absolute truth, and did not hesitate to use them. It is certain that, upon occasion, the writing of prisoners or suspected persons was so artfully imitated as to deceive those best acquainted with it. This was done in the case of father Garnett, whose very peculiar hand was copied so skilfully as to be accepted for his by his most frequent correspondents, theirs being in a like manner reproduced so as to delude him. It is even more important to remember that the government's agents could do what was still more difficult, and throw an air of ingeniousness and simplicity over a carefully concocted tale. On this point I need do no more than quote Mr Jardine's remarks upon the history of the Gunpowder Plot itself:
>
> "No doubt the story which it cost so much pains to distribute, was the result of corresponding care in the manufacture. The same skilful artificier, who had been employed to shape the stories of the treasons of Lopez and the Earl of Essex in Queen Elizabeth's time to suit the objects of the state, was still in the service of the Government; the same statesmen, who directed Bacon to prune the depositions and pervert the facts on the latter of these occasions, was still an active minister of the Crown ... the whole scheme of the *Discourse* [the

169 M.Beardsley, Ibid., p.90.

'King's Book'] is the same as that of the *Declaration of the Earl of Essex's Treasons*, viz., **to surround fiction by undoubted truths with such apparent simplicity and carelessness, but in fact with such consummate art and depth of design, that the reader is beguiled into an unsuspecting belief in the whole narration..."**

We here gather that the official Gunpowder-Plot narrative, the *King's Book*, was cooked up by the same insiders who framed that just and good man, the Earl of Essex, to have him executed!

Gerard's text continues by a further quote from the lawyer David Jardine:[170]

> Of several hundreds of examinations which were taken, two only were published in this narrative [The King's Book], namely a Declaration of Guy Fawkes and a Confession of Thomas Winter. That both of these were carefully settled and prepared for the purpose of publication is not only highly probable from a comparison of them with other statements of the same individuals, which are still extant, but is demonstrated as a fact by the interlineations and alterations observable upon the originals.

It was suspicious, Gerard found, that Wintour's narrative should corroborate that of Faulkes "in particulars which neither of them, nor any of their fellows, thought of mentioning on any other occasion; nay that his relation [i.e., re-telling of the narrative] should agree with this of Faulkes' so closely as to include the statement concerning Owen, which Faulkes never made, but the Government fabricated, and should even make it larger in some important circumstances..."

If they lied about this, Gerard asks, what else did they lie about? His final, damning judgement was -

> **But if this fundamental document be fraudulent, what becomes of the official history of the Gunpowder Plot? It is not merely that the story falls to pieces for want of the bond which has hitherto seemed to coordinate its various parts. If the government adopted such a device as the manufacture of evidence like this, they undeniably had an end in view which only falsehood could secure, and**

170 David Jardine, *A Narrative of the Gunpowder Plot,* 1857.

deliberately set themselves to impose a perversion of history upon the world, and by so doing have furnished against themselves evidence more damning than any other could possibly supply.

We should be alarmed if indeed this skill in the art of deception should *continue to exist* within the fabric of British Intelligence today, whereby the people can be manipulated and deceived for the sake of those in power.

Holbeach: A Modern comparison

After whatever happened - or rather, didn't happen - in London on November 5th, the fleeing plotters found a Catholic hideout at a place called Holbeach not far from Stratford-on-Avon, pursued by the Sheriff of Warwickshire. The next morning (the 8th) they were captured by the Sherriff's men and four of them shot dead, including Robert Catesby and Thomas Percy. Catesby and Percy emerged from the house unarmed and holding between them a crucifix. They attempted to surrender but were shot. One could say this is the one part of the whole drama where something did actually happen. (One could add here the letter delivered to Lord Monteagle on 26th of October as another thing that did, so to speak, actually happen.)

Upon arrival on the 7th of November at Holbeche House, the plotters were allegedly carrying a couple of bags of gunpowder with them, one of which had become damp. They spread out the powder to dry near to the fire and a spark ignited it. Three of them were too close to this powder as it exploded and so were badly burnt and one of them blinded. The powder 'blew up the roof of the house.' Another nearby bag of gunpowder had strangely been put next to the powder spread out to dry near to the fire, and it was miraculously thrown by the explosion though the hole in the roof and into the Courtyard - 'whole and unfired'. Recognizing this, the guilty plotters fell down on their knees, etc. The *King's Book,* narrated all of this as being a proof of Divine Providence

That is a tall story. Its main problem is that gunpowder will not explode if lit, it will merely burn. This impossible account was narrated in the official report which came to be known as the King's Book, *A Discourse of the Manner of the Discovery of the Gunpowder Plot*. Wondered Martyn Beardsley (in his The *Gunpowder Plot Deceit*, p.93), could some of the plotters have been captured and tortured, 'hence the burns and blinding?'

Earlier, Francis Edwards had commented: 'This is one of the strangest incidents in the whole story…It is incredible that gentlemen of the presumed sophistication of those involved should have acted so foolishly, not to say negligently.' (Tesimond, p.133) The source for the story was Sir Edward Coke, who was the judge at the plotters' trial. There were no 'plotters' who confessed to having seen it.

Altogether about eighty men-at arms in the Midlands were involved and that would not have been enough to even think about a rebellion: to quote Francis Edwards again, 'Even allowing for a considerable reduction in the party from its number when it first set out, there could never have been enough to constitute, or even begin, a serious rebellion. This was only the remnant of a company going over to reinforce the English regiment then re-forming in Flanders.' (Ibid, p131). A lot of the story here concerns Guy Fawkes having been a military general over in Flanders, involved in Queen Elizabeth's war between Protestants and Catholics.

The Holbeach story concerns some gunpowder that blows up. It served to counter a risk, that the whole gunpowder story might be disbelieved, or that a challenge would be put out for anyone who had seen the gunpowder barrels to speak up. The story of what had happened at Holbeach became associated with the Plot, the villains and the powder. It provided the notion of an explosion, of something associated with the plotters going bang – even though it was physically impossible.

Through comparison with state-fabricated terror events in this 21st century one may gain a proper framework for evaluating how the Gunpowder plot *worked*. Here are two modern examples, showing the fabric of delusional logic whereby the people of England were conned. The first was a real terror event while the second we may call 'phantom terror.' The latter alludes to an imaginary or constructed event where nobody dies, except the perps. The Gunpowder Plot belongs to this second category. 'Phantom terror' events have the perps either die or be jailed for a long time, so that nobody gets to hear their story.

In the first category terror is generated by the event, whereas for the second type it is the media which drums up the emotions of fear and terror, to an extent that serves to inhibit normal critical thought. The thus-imagined wicked enemy is presented as threatening our whole way of life. The story serves to polarise society and demonise dissidents – Catholics, in the present instance, plus any 'recusants' (those who failed to attend church regularly) and anyone sceptical of the new Stuart monarchy that had just come down from Scotland; it further enables the authorities to have your undivided attention, which they may otherwise find difficult, and last but not least it increases funding for the security services, e.g. the huge stately-home, complete with tennis courts etc., which Cecil constructed for himself in the Strand. The many references to Divine Providence in the official report (the *King's Book*) thereby serve to indicate the British-intel plot design.

Here are the two modern cases.

1. The London bombings of 2005, on July 7th, involved four young 'terrorists' coming down to London from Leeds and blowing up three trains and one London bus. The explosions were real enough, but no witnesses could be found who had seen these four young lads in action on that morning. Even on the number 30 bus that blew up in Tavistock Square, no witness cross-examined, who had been on the bus, could remember the bulky figure of Hasib Hussein as being on it. There was CCTV of him pottering around in Boots the Chemist at King's Cross station, but somehow that was not enough. Nor could the Government release CCTV which should have been able to show the young men from Leeds on that day – or, not until several years later, when people complained about the CCTV looking rather doubtful.

A couple of further events were arranged to reinforce the meme of evil terrorists attempting to blow up London transport tubes and/or buses. These were done soon after the 7/7 event in order that the stories would meld together in the public's mind.

Firstly, Jean-Charles de Menezes, the Brazilian electrician at Stockwell tube station, was pursued down into the underground and onto a train by special agents, probably not London's police, where he was dragged onto the floor of the tube train and pumped full of bullets. The 'team-alpha' woman Cressida Dick who supervised this black op. was duly promoted. No Enquiry was held into that cold-blooded killing of an innocent young man.

A week later, some pops and bangs were heard on the London underground but no-one was hurt, at the same time of the morning as the 7/7 attacks. Events happened as before on three tube trains and one bus and as before, all three tube lines ran though King's Cross. It emerged that the police somehow had foreknowledge and mere hours before the event, the Home Secretary warned that London could face another 'terror onslaught.' The four 'Chappati-bombers' were so to speak caught red-handed. They had rucksacks filled with moist chappati flour, black pepper and maybe some weak hydrogen peroxide. It hardly went bang but some did dribble down onto the tube floor. One was 'caught' on a London bus and others were in trains on the Underground and to that extent it echoed the 7/7 event. Each of the young men got thirty years and Londoners were duly terrorised. Quite what they thought they were doing, no-one will ever know. A long court-case ensued, where one blogger remarked, 'These young men do not appear to be hardened Muslim fanatics, rather tricked, lost souls' – a comment that would apply to most of the patsies recruited for these government terror-ops.

Thus the 7/7 event involved real terror but it had a problem that no 'terrorists' were visible: it was therefore made to merge in the public mind with the 21/7 event shortly after where some alleged perps were visible, at comparable space/time locations, although nobody was then harmed.[171]

2. In 2015 on January 7th an attack on the office of a Paris satire magazine *Charlie Hebdo* supposedly took place. A few days later on January 11th nearly four million demonstrators took to the streets of Paris with 'Je suis Charlie' posters. Having their office blown up did not prevent three million copies of the new issue of their satire journal hitting the streets a week later. One month before this event the bankrupt Charlie Hebdo magazine had been bought up by Edouard Baron do Rothschild, which may help one to appreciate how the whole event was well-organized.

There was a problem in that no-one saw any dead bodies, or blood, or any ambulances or medics turning up, nor later were there any post-

171 NK *Terror on the Tube, Behind the Veil of 7/7 – an Investigation*, 2009, Chapter 11 'Echoes of Phantom Terror.'

mortems or coroner's reports: the event was merely reported. A credibility problem could well develop and so at 8.30 on that same morning a police officer cordoned off a street adjacent to the Charlie Hebdo office, to prepare for a drama. A posse of photographers, gathered on an adjacent rooftop waiting for the show to begin, then filmed a black car stopping in the middle of a road right in front of them, from which a black-clad 'terrorist' emerged. Cue to a policeman seen lying nearby on the pavement, and the 'terrorist' goes over and shoots him in the head at point-blank range using an AK-47 rifle. There was no recoil nor any blood seen and the sound was clearly of a blank being fired, with the policeman's head undamaged. Finally 'blood' appeared on the pavement – the next day! Sceptical discussion forums appearing on the web were quickly deleted.[172]

Why, instead of trying to escape, did the 'bad guys' pull up in front of a posse of photographers and pretend to shoot a policeman on the pavement? That event was we suggest required *because of* the absence of perceived deaths in the main alleged event, at the Charlie Hebdo office. That phoney shootout scene blended together with the main event to ensure that newspapers accepted the narrative, that evil 'terrorists' were killing-people. The *problem* of no visible dead bodies or any explosions was resolved by the secondary event, shortly later.

This 2015 fabricated-terror event has analogies with the Gunpowder Plot, in that no-one died in its main event and the government/police preferred to shoot dead the alleged perpetrators rather than capture them. To quote from my book on the subject:

> The purpose of this terror video sequence is that it made the 'terrorists' visible: no film was available of what had happened around the Charlie Hebdo office, nor were any bodies or blood available to view, so there was an immediate danger of public scepticism. We therefore could be shown bad guys killing a defenceless policeman in the aftermath of that attack, already lying down on the pavement. It served to *confirm the narrative.*'[173]

---

172 The one real death in this story happened on the night of January 7/8, that of a senior police officer Helric Fredou, who was preparing a report of the event. While urgently working through the night to prepare this, he unaccountably had an urge to pick up his gun and shoot himself in the head. Had his report not reached the pre-scripted conclusion of Islamic guilt? His wife refused to believe the 'suicide' verdict.

173 N.K. *False Flags over Europe, A Modern History of State-fabricated Terror* 2020 p.161.

When trauma is imposed upon a populace, the rational faculty is inhibited whereby disparate events can be conjoined together to create the delusional image. These two modern accounts illustrate how the trick is done. *For this reason* it is only in the 21st century, with the great blossoming of state-fabricated terror into a major art-form, conditioning all our perceptions with fear – that the design of the Gunpowder Plot can be properly appreciated.

A couple of centuries ago, an anonymous source reckoned that 'This plot is now pretty well understood not to have been hatched by the Papists, but by an inveterate foe of the Catholics of that day, the famous minister of James ...All well-informed persons at present laugh at the whole of this business.'[174] Today, this may not be a laughing-matter, if indeed the terrible skill in the art of deception *does yet endure*. Take, for example, the Manchester arena bomb-terror event of May, 2017, with a couple of dozen alleged deaths: Richard D. Hall researched this very thoroughly, investigating each family which had allegedly had a victim, and his four-hundred page report amply demonstrated that no-one had really died and that the event was carefully *staged*, set up with actors and dummies.[175] Do we hear any discussion or media evaluation of this major forensic investigation? No, we don't: as if the British public relish or in some way require the hate and fear generated by these fake events.

The word 'theatre' derives from *theos* or *thea,* the gods, i.e. it brings the gods or maybe divine principles onstage whereby we, the audience, are taken through *catharsis* as we empathise with the drama. Whereas, the straight-from-hell *theatre* of state-fabricated terror has a different aim, whereby we lose our humanity and come to distrust our neighbours. It first began four hundred years ago with the Gunpowder Plot.

---

174 'Architect' writing in the Gentleman's Magazine of July 1800 (Gerard, Ibid., p52)
175 R.D.Hall, *Manchester - The Night of the Bang, an Investigation of the 2017 Manchester Arena Incident*, 2018.

21st Century: The Terrible Knowledge

If we look at major European state-fabricated terror events of the 21st century, with English ones here given in red -

* Madrid train bombings, 2004
* **London 7/7 bombings, 2005**
* **Heathrow liquid bomb hoax 2006**
* Crotch bomber at Amsterdam airport, 2009
* Norway Utoya Island massacre, 2011
* **the Woolwich Terror hoax 2013**
* Ukraine MH17 shootdown, 2013
* Paris, Charlie Hebdo 2015
* Bataclan, Paris hit by fictional terror, 2016
* Mock Terror in Brussels airport, 2016
* Nice, Munich & Mossad 2016
* **Phantom terror over Westminster Bridge, 2017**
* **Fake terror at Manchester arena concert, 2017**[176]

- it becomes evident that England has displayed an astonishing priority over the rest of Europe in this diabolical art.[177] Could it be, that its intelligence services still preserve knowledge from 1605 concerning how to deceive and terrorise its own populace? A huge amount of effort goes into organising these complicated deceptions. *To create fear is the aim.* The *Phantom Menace* is thereby conjured up, a menace that serves to promote the 'security' services. Foreign countries are blamed, just as every effort was made in the Gunpowder Plot to blame the Pope and

176 N.K, Ibid. p.16.

177 NB, the Gladio terror-events of the 1980s which plagued Italy and France, progenitors of what has unfolded in his century: see Richard Cottrell, *Gladio, NATO's Dagger at the Heart of Europe,* 2015.

Jesuits. Here is Webster Tarpley's comment on how the Gunpowder Plot *permanently damaged* English culture:

> ... what we're identifying here is a permanent weakness of the English- speaking culture everywhere, because if you've had this fabrication, this orchestrated, manipulated, stage-managed stunt of the Gunpowder Plot, and you've had that made into a religion, that got into the Anglican book of common prayer, and it says in there, and this was up until 1859-1860, every 5th of November, the priest has got to preach on the Gunpowder Plot, you've got to read the Act of Parliament, you've got to go through this whole prayer routine about Gunpowder Treason and Guy Fawkes and the rest of it – it becomes a civic religion. Now when you look at 9/11, there's an attempt to make 9/11 into a civic religion, an ersatz religion, a fake religion, and force people to believe it.

Only one remedy exists for this affliction and that is to bring the whole subject up into our conscious awareness, to discuss it in public and not allow it to remain hidden. Only in secrecy can this black art flourish.

2022 – Tower of London Virtual Reality Drama

The Gunpowder plot immersive experience. A Virtual reality experience of London in 1605. Vaults underground near the Tower of London. History's most famous plot. History's most daring conspiracy. London, 1605. A city divided. The fuse of rebellion is lit. The peace of the nation balances on a knife edge... Step into a world where spies and informants hide in every shadow…: the usual story.

The Dud Gunpowder – Official Record

> 'Receipt for 1,800 lb of Guy Fawkes' gunpowder found' – Telegraph, 4 May 1978.
>
> PRO Debenture books – Septimo die Novembris, 1605, Anno regni R. Jacobi tertio,
>
> Received into his Majesties store within Th'office of Th'ordenaunce from out of the Vault undernethe the Parliament howse Corne

powder XVIII weighte decaied, which was there laid up and placed for the blowing up of the said howse and destruction of the Kings Majestie, the Nobilitie and Commonalitie there assembled.

Receaved the aforesaid cornepowder decaied, XVIII wt.

A separate record shows it cost 15s 6d to move the gunpowder to the Tower.

Dramatis personae

Carleton, Dudley, English diplomat and Secretary of State

Castelmaine, Lord (Roger Palmer) fell victim to trumped-up 'Popish plot' charge.

Catesby, Robert charismatic, Oxford-educated 'leader' of the gunpowder Plotters

Coke, Sir Edward, top judge and lawyer

Cecil, Robert, created Earl of Salisbury in 1605: awarded Order of the Garter in 1606.

Essex, 2nd Earl of, Robert Devereux, 1576-1601

Fawkes, Guido Mercenary soldier

Goodman, Geoffrey, Anglican Bishop of Gloucester, wrote 'The Court of King James'

James I, the new Stuart King, formerly James IV of Scotland

Monteagle, Lord, 4th Baron Monteagle, an English peer.

Northumberland, 9th Earl of, son of Henry 8th, Henry Percy

Percy, Thomas top plotter, Cambridge graduate, served Earl of Northumberland

Wynter, Thomas, plotter whose testimony appeared as the most important

Recommended books:

John Gerard, *What was the Gunpowder Plot? The Traditional Story tested by Evidence,* 1896[178] (also reprinted as *The Gunpowder Plot: 17th century False Flag*, 1897, 2014)

Antonia Frazer *The Gunpowder Plot, Terror and Faith in 1605,* 1996

Francis Edwards, *Guy Fawkes the Real Story of the Gunpowder Plot?* 1969; *The Enigma of the Gunpowder Plot: the 3rd Solution,* 2008.

Richard Dutton, *Ben Jonson, Volpone and the gunpowder Plot,* 2012.

Martyn Beardsley, *The Gunpowder Plot Deceit,* 2018.

David Jardine, *A Narrative of the Gunpowder Plot,* 1857, 2018.

Index

178 A riposte appeared next year by S.R.Gardiner, *What the Gunpowder Plot Was* (1897), to which Gerard replied: *The Gunpowder Plot & the Gunpowder plotters* (1897).

www.ingramcontent.com/pod-product-compliance
Lightning Source LLC
Chambersburg PA
CBHW040227170726
48295CB00014B/836

9781739999445